ONE HOUSE

ONE HOUSE

The Battle of Adwa 1896—100 Years

Pamela S. Brown and Fassil Yirgu
Editors

Nyala Publishing
Chicago Illinois

Printed in the United States of America.

Nyala Publishing
1250 W. Addison
Chicago, IL 60613
312-883-9818

Articles by Richard Pankhurst first appeared in the October 1957 issue of the *Ethiopian Observer*, Addis Ababa.

cover art: Fasil Dawit
book design: Pamela S. Brown

ISBN 0-9642068-1-1

Contents

Illustrations

Preface

I grew up in the United States in a time when everything seemed possible. Relative prosperity produced a feeling of generosity toward others and I was luckily raised in an atmosphere of tolerance and openness to the new and the unfamiliar. Times have indeed changed. It seems that everyone is ready to retreat to their own small group and has forgotten the once noble goal of one world.

I along with most of you have noted the increasingly negative images of Africans in the media over the past decade or so. It is alarming to find that many people do not question these portrayals. Knowing as I do many Ethiopians and other Africans, I can read between the lines of some of these reports. But, as psychologists have found, if you hear something enough it is pretty hard to not believe any of it.

The 100 year anniversary of the Battle of Adwa in which Italian (European) colonial ambitions were first thwarted comes only once. But this has been an opportunity to not only tell a story that most of the history books have forgotten, but an opportunity to apply the lessons we can learn from the event. It is a time to celebrate the value of common cause, common commitment and common action. It is a time to recall that success comes because of the cooperation of people who could have looked at their differences, but instead looked at their similarities. And it is a time to acknowledge that we all live in *One House* and stop trying to move out.

This book seeks to show how a historic event has influenced generations of people interested in Ethiopia and how it can serve as continued inspiration.

There are many ways to understand the history of an event such as Adwa. Details of the battle and its repercussions in Europe led to consequences to nations and their political relations. But history is also revealed through looking at social interactions, symbolism and cultural affects. Many contributors of different backgrounds have helped to create this fuller understanding.

Donald L. Levine, Ethiopia's foremost sociologist tells us why the Battle of Adwa's most significant achievement was multiethnic cooperation.

Tsegaye Gabre-Medhin, Ethiopia's Poet Laureate, questions whether Ethiopia has learned the lessons of Adwa.

Ayele Bekerie who teaches African Studies, tells us how the Battle of Adwa has served as inspiration to the pan-African movement and countless writers, artists, painters and leaders.

Teshale Tibebu who teaches African History, provides background on the nation-building that paved the way for Emperor Menelik's Ethiopia.

Fikre Tolossa, poet/playwright/teacher, retells the story of the Battle of Adwa in traditional epic style.

Richard Pankhurst, Ethiopia's foremost historian, provides the facts—how the battle was fought, who was involved, how England reacted and the effects in Europe and Africa.

Amare Tegbaru, writer of historical fiction, retells the story of the Battle of Adwa as oral history in Ethiopia today.

Afework Tekle, Ethiopia's Master Artist, contributes modern portraits of Ethiopian patriots.

Fasil Dawit, an artist who spent weeks in Adwa itself, provides cover art and realistic scenes of the common and the glorious to make us feel that we are there.

Throughout the book, artists from 1896 to today, representing both African and Western styles, continue to draw inspiration from Adwa and reinterpret it for us.

Perhaps the most gratifying result of this project is the enthusiastic individuals from many countries who have supported the idea. Together we are building a network of like-minded individuals who can spread the message of positive cooperation we hope to engender.

Special thanks go to Alula Wassé who shared his archives of etchings and news articles and to Manny Dominguez for invaluable help in computer reproduction of all art.

Pamela S. Brown

Introduction

One morning I woke up, suddenly unsure of whether any of us could go on living and reasoning together. I had always believed that we would understand each other better over time. I wasn't prepared for the present ethnic politics and degeneration of human relationships in our world. But, then, wonderful childhood memories of my family, friends and all those I grew up with made me think again. And I found hope.

I was compelled to create *One House* to not only highlight and draw upon the best traditions of African peoples, but to remind us of universal values and skills we used to have, skills that can lead us today to new and creative approaches to reaching our goals. The many views of the story of Adwa can allow us to enter the mindset of their times, to learn about their self-reliance and the methods that contributed to their achievements.

One House: The Battle of Adwa—100 Years is the story of how one sovereign African state responded to European colonialism and conquest, retaining their independence and proving their ability to build coalition and consensus. The heroes and heroines of Adwa succeeded because they had a worthy goal, a strong commitment and a clear plan of action. That lesson is one we could all use.

A traditional society and early civilization—whether in Africa, Asia, America or Latin America—gives you a living sense of human history, a view of thousands rather than tens of years. As the home of our human ancestors, the 3.5 million-year-old Dinqnesh reminds us of common roots. Early civilizations—of every nationality—were based on what was best for the community as a whole. Likewise, modern cultures can benefit from the emphasis on community, but remain aware that the community has and must grow in inclusiveness.

What are the ingredients needed to achieve a desired end? In the case of the Ethiopia of the last century, the goal—sovereignty and independence—was unquestionable. When Ethiopia's sovereignty was threatened by Italy, after numerous efforts to end misunderstanding failed, Emperor Menelik II of Ethiopia and the regional leaders, brought together by Menelik's vision, decided together to expel the invading Italians.

The second requirement is to create strong commitment. The commitment of the Ethiopian people to remain sovereign was reaffirmed by the Battle of Adwa. The Italians, hoping to take advantage of regional, ethnic and religious differences among Ethiopians, had devised a strategy to divide and conquer. Emperor Menelik succeeded in gathering a force of 100,000 to resist the Italian invasion by helping regional leaders to balance their competing interests for the greater good. This resulting success was beyond the expectations of anyone outside of Ethiopia. As now, the European newspapers of 100 years ago created only negative images of Africa and Africans for their readers.

Just as in Ethiopia, indepence has required commitment for the peoples of Africa, Asia, Latin America and the United States. In America, the struggle of workers to form unions, of women and African-Americans to achieve equality, of cross-sections for free speech, freedom from nuclear threat and a livable environment have also followed the same path.

The long and difficult struggle of the people of South Africa to win their political rights against colonialism, racism and apartheid was made possible through coalitions. Throughout Africa are many examples of heroic fights for independence. Patrice Lumumba, the Congolese revolutionary who stood up to colonialism, awoke passions all over Africa. These movements won hearts and minds of many, making them cross traditional boundaries of nationality, race and class to join together. Many lost their lives, were imprisoned and suffered innumerable personal hardships as well as risking livelihood.

Vision combined with commitment was essential, but strategy made the difference between defeat and victory at Adwa. Menelik and the regional leaders were more effective and better tacticians. And Menelik had the additional advantage of moral leadership. His proclamation of war is an example. Short and decisive, there was no inflammatory reference to race, nor mention of names. This African emperor was also gracious in victory. He wrote the Italians that he was very sorry to be forced to engage in a battle that caused the death of so many.

As history, *One House* tries to achieve what all writers of history hope for—the celebratation of the victory of individuals and leaders and their special achievement. In the case of Adwa, this special achievement was multiethnic cooperation. The spirit of Adwa can be an inspiration to minimize difference to reach consensus for desired goals.

If in any way this book causes one person to hate another, indeed I have failed. Rather I wish to awaken that longing for community and progress and a model that might help its achievement. On the other hand if *One House* in some small way can help motivate even one person to devise a new method to tackle the problems of our time, indeed our job is done.

Finally on behalf of myself and Nyala Publishing I want to thank all who contributed material to this book and to commemorate the centennial of the Battle of Adwa by saluting those who have sacrificed themselves for the independence of Ethiopia. They are always in our hearts.

Fassil Yirgu

The Battle of Adwa as a "Historic" Event

Donald N. Levine

There are three reasons why we commonly refer to some happening as a historic event: either it occurs for the first time, it has significant consequences or it is symbolically important. As a *first time event*, Emperor Menelik's cession of the Bogos highlands to Italy in 1889 has been described as historic—as the first time an Ethiopian ruler voluntarily relinquished territory to a foreign power. In the same vein, Abebe Bikila's victory in the marathon race at the 1960 Olympics in Rome was historic—as the first time an Ethiopian won a gold medal.

We also designate events as historic when their *consequences significantly alter* the shape of subsequent *history*. The conversion of King Ezanas to Christianity in the mid-fourth century was historic in this sense because it redirected Ethiopia's cultural development. Similarly, the protection given to disciples of the Prophet Muhammad by the Ethiopian king in the seventh century was historic. It led Muhammad to advise his followers to spare Ethiopia from the jihad of Islamic expansion that took place soon after. Likewise, the killing of Emperor Yohannes IV by Sudanese Mahdists in 1889 was historic because it opened the way to the ascendance of an emperor from Shoa.

Even when events have no significant direct consequences, we tend to call them historic when they *symbolize* important national or universal human ideals. The suicide of Emperor Tewodros II had little political consequence—his rule was over, whether or not he was captured alive by the British—but it came to symbolize a preference for death over demeaning captivity. The speech of Emperor Haile Selassie I to the League of Nations in 1937 is often called a historic address, even though it did nothing to change the course of history. It did, however, come to represent the moral weakness of Western democracies in the face of fascist expansionism and the need for a stronger world organization empowered to provide collective security.

The Battle of Adwa in 1896 qualifies as a historic event in all three senses of the term. As a historic "first," it represented the first time since the beginning of European imperial expansion that a nonwhite nation had defeated a European power.

The Battle of Adwa in 1896 had two fateful consequences—the preservation of Ethiopia's independence from Italian colonization and the confirmation of Italy's control over the part of the country Italy had named Eritrea in 1890. Both consequences had repercussions throughout the twentieth century. Italy experienced her defeat at Adwa as intensely humiliating and that humiliation became a national trauma that demagogic leaders strove to avenge. It also played no little part in motivating Italy's retaliatory adventure in 1935. On the other hand, Italy's continued occupation of Eritrea gave her a convenient springboard from which to launch that invasion. A generation later tensions stemming from the protracted division of historic Ethiopia into two parts—one under European governance, one under the Ethiopian Crown—culminated in a long civil war and the eventual secession of Eritrea as an independent state in 1993.

In addition to these actual historic consequences, the Battle of Adwa acquired symbolic significance of many kinds. In some instances this symbolism itself came to exert a certain influence on the course of events.

Adwa's Symbolism in Other Countries

In Europe, the short-term symbolic significance of the Ethiopian defeat of Italy in 1896 was that it initiated a rethinking of the Europeans' image of Africa and Africans. During the nineteenth century Africa was viewed in increasingly derogatory terms, as a continent of people so primitive they were fit only for European rule. Ethiopia did not escape such swipes. British officers called Ethiopia a nation of savages. Italian officials described it as "a nation of primitive tribesmen led by a barbarian." The British Foreign Office supported the provocative move of giving Zula to Italy, expecting Emperor Yohannes to protest by attacking and then easily punishing him for imagining Ethiopians were equal to white men. Kaiser Wilhelm responded to Emperor Menelik's announcement of his accession to the throne with insulting language. The stunning victory at Adwa required Europeans to take Ethiopia and Africa more seriously. It not only initiated a decade of negotiations with European powers in which nine border treaties were signed. It made Europeans begin to reconsider their prejudices against Africans. It came to symbolize a rising awareness among Europeans of African political resources and ambitions and an increasing recognition of indigenous African cultural accomplishments.

In Japan, Ethiopia became appreciated as the first non-Caucasian power to defeat Europeans, an achievement the

Afework Tekle

Menelik at the Battle of Adwa, 1896 A.D.

Japanese were to duplicate in warfare against Russia in 1904. This appreciation led to a sense of affinity that bore fruit for decades. Ethiopian intellectuals looked to Japan as a model for modernizing their ancient monarchy; the Meiji Constitution served as a model for the Ethiopian Constitution of 1931. When Italy invaded Ethiopia again in the mid-1930s, Japanese citizens (if not the regime formally) expressed solidarity with Ethiopians, sending shipments of many thousands of swords to help them in their plight.

In Africa, the Battle of Adwa inspired other kinds of symbolism. For a number of colonized Africans, the Ethiopian victory at Adwa represented the possibility of future emancipation. Black South Africans of the Ethiopian Church came to identify with the Christian kingdom in the Horn, a connection, which led South African leader James Dwane to write Menelik for help in caring for the Christian communities of Egypt and Sudan. The victory at Adwa made Ethiopia visible as a beacon of African independence. This position inspired figures like Nnamdi Azikiwe in Nigeria, Kwame Nkrumah in Ghana and Jomo Kenyatta in Kenya in the early years of the African independence movement, as well as leaders in the West Indies such as George Padmore and Marcus Garvey in Jamaica.

Adwa as a Symbol of Ethiopia's Tradition of Independence

Within Ethiopia itself Adwa symbolized many things. Some had positive consequences for her development while others did not. Internally, as abroad, it symbolized Ethiopia's proud commitment to freedom from foreign domination. Of the many emblems of Ethiopia's historic independence, Adwa is perhaps the most visible and the most dramatic. The spirit of Ethiopia's defiant protection of its land from outsiders manifests itself in many forms. There is the apocryphal story of Emperor Tewodros ordering the boots of some visitors washed before they embarked on a ship back to Europe, and then saying: "Far more precious than jewels is a single drop of Ethiopian soil." There was the refrain I used to hear young braves chant at festive times, jabbing dula sticks up and down as they danced and sang:

Min alle Teqel, min alle? Agaren le-sew, agaren-le sew, al-setim alle.

or

ምን አለ ጠቅል ምን አለ? አገሬን ለሰው አልሰጥም አለ

What did Teqel [Haile Selassie's horse-name] say, what did he say? I won't give my country to foreigners, that's what he said.

With respect to Menelik's reputation, it partly overcame the resentments he had stirred up by relinquishing Bogos to Italy in exchange for help against his competitors in Tigray.

As a historic assertion of Ethiopia's independence, Adwa also reverberated with memories of Ethiopia's experience as a long-lived independent polity. Its symbolism thereby encompassed a layer of meaning that alluded to the historic depth of the Ethiopian nation. It revived memories of earlier achievements and yearnings.

At the same time, Adwa may have served to give Ethiopians a false sense of confidence about their position in the modern world. In showing themselves and the world that they could defeat a European invader with their own resources, the 1896 campaign may have led them to think that their traditional resources would be adequate in an era of war waged with tanks and airplanes. It gave encouragement to isolationist and conservative strains that were deeply rooted in Ethiopian culture, strengthening the hand of those who strove to keep Ethiopia from adopting techniques imported from the modern West—resistance with which both emperors Menelik and Ras Tafari/Haile Selassie would have to contend.

Adwa as a Symbol of Multiethnic Cooperation

The symbolism of multiethnic collaboration evoked by the Battle of Adwa has been less visible than its role in symbolizing Ethiopia's tradition of independence. Yet in some ways the former was the most remarkable and meaningful aspect of the entire episode. Although members of different ethnic, religious and regional groups had been interacting regularly in Ethiopia for more than 2,000 years—through trade, intermarriage, common ritual observances, pilgrimages and political competition—from the perspective of Ethiopian history, Adwa offers the most dramatic instance of multiethnic collaboration before the twentieth century. This is because it gave expression

Ethiopian soldiers from all corners of the empire

Fasil Dawit 1995

to a great outpouring of national patriotism, foreshadowing the great patriotic struggles of 1935–41. Even from the perspective of modern world history, Adwa represented a relatively rare struggle for national independence waged by a coalition of diverse ethnic groups.

Twenty-five years earlier, Adwa had been the scene of a protracted battle between Dejazmatch Kasa, who later became Emperor Yohannes IV, and the reigning emperor, Tekla-Giorgis II, formerly Wag Shum Gobeze. What the 1871 Battle of Adwa symbolized was the age-old struggle among different regional and ethnic groups for dominance. Yohannes, like Tewodros II before him, came to the throne determined to reunify the empire which had been fragmented following the invasion of Ahmad Gragn and subsequent divisive developments. Although Yohannes did not live to see it, the 1896 Battle of Adwa was a tribute to his vision and to his thoughtful determination to unify Ethiopia while respecting the local jurisdictions of regional kings and lords so long as they remained faithful to the national crown.

Those who would deny Ethiopia's long existence as a multiethnic society must be embarrassed by the facts of the Adwa experience. If the empire consisted of nothing but a congeries of separate tribal and regional groups, how then account for the courageous collaboration of 100,000 troops from dozens of ethnic groups from all parts of the country? How then explain the spirited national patriotism of such diverse leaders as Ras Alula, Ras Mangesha and Ras Sebhat of Tigray, Dejazmatch Bata of Akale Guzae, Wag Shum Guangul of Lasta, Ras Mikael of Wallo, Negus Tekla-Haimanot of Gojjam, Ras Gobena and Dejazmatch Balcha of the Mecha Oromo, Ras Wole of the Yajju Oromo, Fitawrari Tekla of Wellega, Ras Makonnen of Harar, as well as Fitawrari Gebeihu (who died fighting at Adwa) and Ras Abate of Shoa?

Of course, deeply rooted antagonisms and persistent rivalries among different factions beset Ethiopia throughout the nineteenth century. And yet, as historian Sven Rubenson has written, "at the crucial moment, Menelik commanded the loyalty of every important chief in the country." The battle of Adwa became and remains the most outstanding symbol of what, a half century later, a British colonel would describe as the "mysterious magnetism" that holds Ethiopia together.

tending the Ethiopian wounded — Fasil Dawit 1995

Adwa—What For?

Tsegaye Gabre-Medhin
Ethiopia's Poet Laureate

Adwa still rises high
on this roof of Africa. Ethiopia.
But we! What do we want
to remember Adwa for?

Adwa extends itself beyond time
to caress our present shameful presence.
Adwa. Symbolic banner of the indomitable.
The spirit of the substantive men of all times.
Adwa. Still rising above ominous clouds.
Adwa. Epicenter of the black world epic,
But we! Midgets
in the comfortable shades
of America's fast food fabrics.
We! Born of the great names
but ourselves of no significance,
What do we want to remember Adwa for?

Does the glory of Adwa
glow, from their heroic past for you?
Does Menelik the black man's miracle
tower for you above the statuette
of that colonial Italian wolf?

Adwa. Monumental memory of black honor.
Adwa. Collective memory of our giants.
Adwa. Footprint of Ethiopia's pharaonic ancestors,
of Cheops to Thutmosis, Mecha to Ramses,
Soboq to Kaleb, Tewodros to Menelik,
Adwa, the Atbara of Ada Awa
of the Earth Mother of all mankind,
Adwa, of the true sons of Ethiop,
Symbol of the aboriginal Kamits,
of the heroic sons and daughters of Africa,
of the builders of Nagada, of Atbara,
of Meroe, of Saba Land, of Adulis, of Aksum,
who first fathered the pyramids
and the Pharaonic wonders of all times,
but we! What do we want
to remember Adwa for?

Adwa. Supreme architect of black honor,
an African glory over European colonialism
and a memory of shame to world fascism,
to secessionist tribalism,
and to bloody minded banda-ism!
Adwa. The African code of distinction
inherited from this land of the beginning of man,
Adwa. Symbol of tomorrow's sunrise
Even on this Horn of Africa,
Adwa. The hidden secret of black unity
warning us against horning each other
into the kind of Red Indian extinction,
Adwa. Banner of black success
rising here on the cradle of mankind
and still shining to warn the beasts away,
Adwa. Shimmering on this roof of Africa. Ethiopia.
But we! The deformed midgets
crawling under imperial world towers,
what do we want to remember Adwa for?

Addis Ababa, Ethiopia
October 14, 1995

Fasil Dawit 1995

families sharing a meal in camp

How Africa Defeated Europe

Ayele Bekerie

Introduction

One hundred years ago, at the height of the so-called scramble for Africa by European colonial powers, the Ethiopian army led by Emperor Menelik and Empress Taitu Bitul won a military and psychological victory against the Italian army. It was at the Battle of Adwa on March 1, 1896 that the world witnessed the defeat of a European army. It was at the Battle of Adwa that Africans began to reverse the colonial scheme concocted by Europeans at the infamous Berlin Conference of 1884–85. It was at the Battle of Adwa that Africans expressed the extent of their convictions and determination to remain a free people. It was at the Battle of Adwa that Africans were able to show their willingness to come together in defense of their motherland and cultures, regardless of their religious, ethnic and linguistic affiliations.

Moslems and Christians, Oromos and Amharas, lowlanders and highlanders, Northerners and Southerners, women and men marched together, fought together and made an enormous sacrifice to uphold their natural rights to remain a free and sovereign people.

Adwa reflects, therefore, the essence of an Ethiopian and African identity. It forms the basis of an African identity because the Adwa conflict was a deliberate response to an imperial European scheme of global expansion and domination. It took place at a time when Europe was implementing its grand design of divide and rule throughout the continent of Africa. The outcome of the battle shattered Europe's false claim of supremacy and invincibility. Further, the victory was instrumental in the initiation and promotion of pan-African movements and organizations in the African world.

Adwa defined the essence of national unity. Adwa demonstrated to the whole world what the so-called forgotten people can do to defend their natural rights of independence and to show the depth of their sense of being. Adwa also revealed that Ethiopia's source of greatness lies in the conviction that freedom belongs to everyone. And, Adwa shines especially brilliantly in the annals of world history because of the critical roles played by its leaders who represented people of various linguistic, religious and economic backgrounds and yet united to defend their country and their freedom. Adwa was also a place for women leaders, such as Empress Taitu Bitul, who led her own battalion to the battlefield in 1896.

One of the most remarkable stories of the confrontation between the Ethiopians and the Italians illuminates the power of language. The Italians, alongside their colonial counterparts in Europe, drafted and submitted treaties of acquiescence and surrender to the unsuspecting Ethiopians. The trick, of course, did not work with Ethiopia. As an independent country with its own writing system—incidentally, older than the Italian system—it, too, drafted a treaty of peace with Italy in its own language. According to the Ethiopian/Amharic version of the 1889 Wuchale Treaty, the Ethiopians would enjoy peaceful cooperation between two sovereign countries. The Italians, employing their own interpretation, used the treaty as a pretext for colonization. As Empress Taitu put it,

> *the treaty as it is written in our language, is an affirmation of our independence and dignity. Ethiopia shall never be a protectorate of any other power.*

The Ethiopian language not only affirmed the depth of Ethiopian philosophy, culture and history, it served as proof of Italian treachery. The failure to reach peaceful agreement regarding the interpretations of the Wuchale Treaty ultimately was resolved on the battlefield on March 1, 1896 at the Battle of Adwa. The Ethiopians achieved not only a victory in the field but also an affirmation of their right to define and communicate in their own languages. It was a victory that ushered in a new beginning in the struggle against European colonialism. It was a victory that signaled the end of the prolonged European domination of Africa, Asia and the Americas. It was a victory for African languages and cultures.

The independence of Ethiopia had been challenged by European powers since the 1884–85 Berlin Conference. The Italians' desire to conquer and colonize Ethiopia started in 1882 and culminated when they were routed from the country and the Horn of Africa in 1941. In this sixty-year period, Italians invaded Ethiopia seven times. For the most part, Ethiopia successfully defended her sovereignty until losing ground between 1935 and 1941.

Adwa was the most famous battle, for it shattered the myth of white supremacy. Adwa's victory not only affirmed Ethiopia's sovereignty but it also "gave to the oppressed Africans new hope of freedom," according to Chris Prouty in *Empress Taytu and Menelik II: Ethiopia 1883–1910.* Notes

J.A. Rogers in *The Real Facts About Ethiopia*, "The victory amazed Europe and heartened African people everywhere." Four years later, in 1900, the first pan-African Conference was held. Emperor Menelik was asked to lead an international organization of African people.

One of my favorite drawings shows the victorious leaders of the Battle of Adwa. These Ethiopians came from different regions of the country, accepting the call made by their emperor. This illustration, at right, shows the leaders in their battle regalia—all barefooted. Although an army with a lesser level of technological sophistication and armament, it still managed to dismantle the whole notion of European supremacy as stated at the Berlin Conference.

It is because of this achievement that we see Adwa as a great symbol of resistance, unity, cultural integrity, African intelligence and African values. Adwa taught a lesson to imperial European expansionists; it forced them to acknowledge the existence of other cultures. Moreover, Adwa may have paved the way for the establishment of an international understanding and respect for the political, economic and cultural rights of all the world's peoples.

Ethiopia's Symbolic Significance

> *The Ethiopians conceived themselves to be of greater antiquity than any other nation, and it is probable that, born under the sun's path, its warmth may have ripened them earlier than other men. They supposed themselves to be the inventors of worship, of festivals, of solemn assemblies, of sacrifice, and every religious practice.*

These glorious words were composed by the great historian of antiquity, Diodorous Siculus. It is the depth and richness of Ethiopia's cultures that served as a rallying point for people to set aside their internal differences to unite for freedom and independence.

Ethiopia evokes passion, deep sentiments, and instant love and affection in almost all people of the African world. Among others, Ethiopia inspired poets Langston Hughes and Claude McKay; novelist John O. Killens; journalist J.A. Rogers; historians John Henrik Clarke and Carter G. Woodson; nationalists like Queen Mother Moore (the immortal and the

from Guèbré Sellassié *Chronique du règne de Menelik II: 1830–1896* Paris 1930–31 *Ethiopian warriors in ceremonial dress* courageous elder woman who gave a very moving and inspiring speech on October 16, 1995 at the Million Man March in Washington, D.C.), Marcus Garvey, and Kwame Nkrumah (the first president of Ghana and a founder of the Organization of African Unity in 1963); pan-Africanists George Padmore and W.E.B. DuBois; minister Adam Clayton Powell, Jr. of the Abyssinian Baptist Church of Harlem, New York; and artists Romare Bearden and Paul Robeson.

Ethiopia's symbolism is broad and distinct. Ancient Ethiopia —geographically speaking—was almost synonymous with Africa. Ethiopia is biblical, legendary and mythical. Moreover, Ethiopia is the home of one of the oldest existing cultures of the world.

Professor Ali Mazrui, in an interview conducted at Cornell University, stated that "the name Ethiopia—biblically speaking—was equated with the name Africa—land of black people." He further pointed out that ancient Libya was as large as ancient Ethiopia and yet Libya never fired the imagination of the African diaspora as did Ethiopia.

According to an Ethiopian tradition, the word *Ethiopia* is derived from *Ethiopis*, a name of an Ethiopian king, the seventh in the ancestral line. The Ethiopian Book of Aksum identifies Itiopis (ኢትዮጲስ) as the twelfth king of Ethiopia. Etymologically, the word *Ethiopia*, particularly the prefix *Eth*, in some Ethiopian traditions, is traced to *Itan* (እጣን), a Ge'ez/Amharic word for incense. The term may refer to the land of incense or the sacred land—a possible reference to the Ethiopian plateau. The term is also used in association with or as a substitute for well known terms from African antiquity, such as *Kush* and *Punt*.

Ethiopia's currently estimated sixty million people constitute more than seventy sociolinguistic groupings. Ninety percent of them are engaged in agriculture. The Oromos, 40 percent of the total population, are the largest sociolinguistic group. Recent works have established links between the Oromos and the ancient Egyptians of the dynastic period, suggesting a presence in the region as old as the Aksumites, the Amharas, the Bejas and the Agaus. The Oromos encompass a vast array of regions, religions and economic activities. For instance, while those who live in the lowlands espouse mostly Islam, the highland dwellers have incorporated Christianity into their traditional belief systems. The Amharas and the Tigreans, the second largest constituents, together formed the elites who ruled Ethiopia for more than a millennium. Southern and eastern Ethiopia is home for people of the Wallamos, Gurages, Somalis and Afars, just to mention a few.

The mobile nature of the Ethiopian feudal monarchy—most of Ethiopian history—and the constant infiltrations, invasions and temporary occupations by various non-African forces transformed the country into a land of multinational and multicultural groupings. Cross-fertilization of cultures, languages and belief systems resulted from the dynamic interactions among people for a length of time that can be matched only by the Chinese or the Persians. The various cultures fused and sifted into a unified identity interwoven with elements of diversity.

Ethiopia's long-sustained independence, unique and sixteen-hundred-year-old Christian tradition, its references in the Bible and ancient classic literatures, and its acknowledged role in the formative period of Islam generated a powerful image to African people throughout the world. The aspiration for freedom linked the enslaved, colonized and oppressed Africans to Ethiopia. Ethiopia became a sacred symbol of the African people's yearning for creative and free existence. Virginia Lee Jacobs articulates this symbolism in her book *Roots of Ras Tafari*. She writes that Ethiopia is

1. a symbol for Africa's struggle for independence from European colonialism;
2. the shrine enclosing the last sacred spark of African political freedom;
3. the impregnable rock of African resistance against white invasions; and
4. a living symbol, an incarnation of African independence.

Ethiopia, in short, has been a constant theme in the thoughts and imaginings of Africans from the Americas to southern Africa. Ethiopia provided the symbol for both nationalist and pan-Africanist perceptions. For instance, the 1900–45 pan-African congresses regularly issued statements that emphasized solidarity with Haiti, Ethiopia and Liberia, thereby affirming the importance of defending the sovereignty and independence of African and Caribbean states.

The Ras Tafari (Rasta) movement started in Jamaica in 1932. Today it is a synthesis of Ethiopia's symbolic value combined with its struggle for freedom and race pride. It is a culturally powerful movement with worldwide influence and acceptance. Reggae music was born out of the Rasta movement and has become one of the most passionate and melodic voices of African people.

The most common and popular tricolors of the flags of independent African countries—or the costumes of African people during the annual Carnival in Brooklyn, New York; Toronto, Canada; London, England; and Port-Au-Spain, Trinidad and Tobago—are green, yellow and red. It is perhaps not merely coincidental that more than twenty African and Caribbean countries have these tricolors in their own national flags. They are also in homes of many African people. Their decorative and philosophical meaning is displayed in mini-flags, belts, caps, hats, wall hangings and other artifacts. The national images of these countries and millions of African people throughout the world are linked with the national image of Ethiopia. Ethiopia's green, yellow, and red flag (ሰንደቅዓላማ) symbolizes the African world quest for identity, freedom and political power.

Most pan-African writers define or identify Ethiopia as the land of African people, the land of the Kushites and the original birthplace of the Nile Valley civilizations. Thus, Ethiopia is recognized as a significant symbol of African people's struggle for self-determination, cultural autonomy and independence.

Ancient Ethiopia

Ethiopia, thou land of our fathers,
Thou land where the gods loved to be,
As storm cloud at night sudden gathers
Our armies come rushing to thee.
We must in the fight be victorious,
When swords are thrust outward to glean;
For us will the vict'ry be glorious
When led by the red, black and green ....

This elegant piece of poetry is an excerpt from the Universal Ethiopian Anthem of the Universal Negro Improvement Association, founded and led by Marcus Garvey. Garvey was able to bring the Ethiopian theme into the common discourse of his followers—five million strong in the United States and

Map of Africa

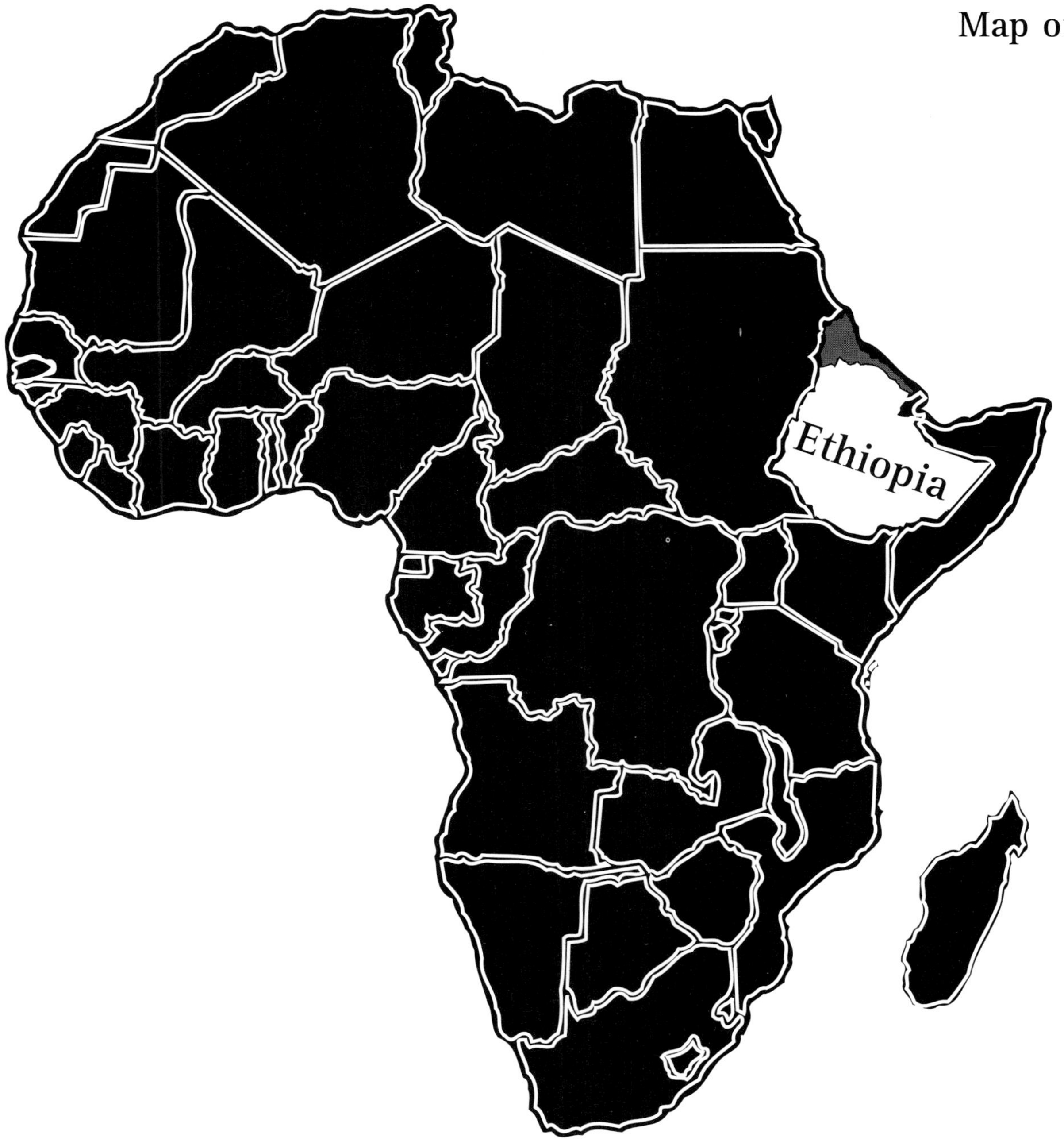

the Caribbean. Since antiquity, Ethiopia has borne great meaning for the African world as a whole. The most cherished quotation from the Bible among African people is the quotation from Psalms 68:31:

> *... Ethiopia shall soon stretch forth her hands to God.*

The biblical prophecy concerning Ethiopia was incorporated into African social, religious, cultural, political and economic movements. From the Universal Negro Improvement Association to the Abyssinian Baptist Church of Harlem; from the Ethiopian church of South Africa to the Rastafarian movement of the Caribbean, the name Ethiopia is invoked with reverence and pride. I think Bernard Magubane put it best when he stated that for a people whose history had been deliberately starved of legend, Ethiopia linked the African to the glory of ancient times.

William Leo Hansberry, eminent African American historian and Ethiopianist scholar, referred to ancient Ethiopia as "the original Eden of humankind." According to J.A. Rogers, Ethiopia was believed by most ancient scholars to have been the first of the nations and the mother of civilization. This statement is not surprising given the findings of paleontologists who discovered perhaps the earliest human-like fossil remains, Dinqnesh (also called Lucy), in the Afar region of eastern Ethiopia.

Arnold Herman Heeren, one of the few factual Africanist scholars, wrote:

> *Except the Ethiopians there is no aboriginal people of Africa with so many claims upon our attention as the Ethiopians; from the remotest times to the present, one of the most celebrated and the most mysterious of nations. In the earliest traditions of nearly all the most civilized nations of antiquity, the name of the distant people is found. The annals of the Egyptian priests were full of them; the nations of inner Asia on the Euphrates and the Tigris have interwoven the fictions of Ethiopia with their own traditions of the conquests and wars of their heroes, and poised equally remote, they glimmer in Greek mythology.*

Fasil Dawit 1995

Menelik's soldiers taking the Italians prisoner

feeding the captured prisoners Fasil Dawit 1995

This eloquent narration of the ancient world of Ethiopia has been a source of citations and inspiration by African people in their struggle to regain their freedom. It is indeed a narration of upliftment and reassertion of Africa's dignity and pride. The late author Sony Labou Tansi of Congo Brazzaville saw ancient Ethiopia as a basis to relink African contemporary "history of defeatisms" to the ancient glory of the past. Africa's past goes beyond the "Atlantic Slave Trade," "Slave Coasts," "Slave Plantations in the New World," "Indirect British Rule," "Share Cropping" and all the other socioeconomic structures imposed upon African people by Europeans. These are terminologies and phrases constructed to perpetuate the European cultural and economic hegemony over African people and resources. Frederich Hegel's contention of a vacuous African past found its indisputable refutation in the rediscovery and repossession of the ancient glory that was truly African. The glory once found in the African bush was transported to European museums, palaces and other governmental and private institutions.

Mussolini, in his attempt to vindicate the Italian army vanquished at the Battle of Adwa, invaded Ethiopia in 1935. The invasion and subsequent five-year occupation provided cover for the most systematic destruction of ancient Ethiopian glory. Mussolini was responsible for the burning of manuscripts. He ordered his army to uproot and transport the Aksum stele, the most impressive symbol of the ancient Aksumite civilizations, to Rome. To date, the stele has not been returned to Ethiopia. What a way to restore the ancient Roman glory—by decorating Rome with a cultural artifact of no meaning beyond war booty!

Ancient Ethiopia and its glory, apart from its restorative and inspirational value for African personality and national identity, became a foundation and a reference point to pan-African movements and organizations throughout the African world. Given the many references to it in so many circles, it is fair to say that Ancient Ethiopia was a catalyst for reputable and historic movements such as Garveyism, Rastafarianism and Ethiopianism from Harlem to Johannesburg. The great pan-African leader Marcus Garvey said it best when he declared:

> *We see our God through our own spectacles. We believe in the God of Ethiopia ... the one God of all ages.*

Post-Adwa Ethiopia

As much as ancient Ethiopia inspired pan-Africanist movements and organizations, post-Adwa Ethiopia's history is significant in anticolonial movements and the rebirth of pan-Africanism. Post-Adwa Ethiopia, formed by forging five separate kingdoms—Tigray, Gojjam, Kaffa, Harar and Shoa—was brought to the African world's attention in 1896 when Ethiopia, an African country, defeated Italy, a European country, at the Battle of Adwa.

Post-Adwa Ethiopia sought partnership and alliance with sovereign nations. She signed bilateral treaties with France, England and Italy, beginning in 1889. While Ethiopia regarded these treaties as diplomatic and peaceful means of preserving her sovereignty and independence, the Europeans, particularly Italy, considered the treaties tactical weapons to colonize Ethiopia. As a result, emperors Menelik and Haile Selassie had to expend considerable energy and resources to ward off European colonial ambitions for Ethiopia.

European powers challenged Ethiopia's independence from the time of the 1885 Berlin Conference. Italy, France and England were fierce competitors in carving Ethiopia into their spheres of influence. These colonial powers signed treaties, colluded and collided with one another in an attempt to colonize Ethiopia. For instance, they signed a treaty in 1906 establishing their respective shares of Ethiopia. The treaty kept the three contending powers from unilaterally occupying Ethiopia.

Italy however long claimed "complete right" over Ethiopia and sought to exercise this right through various schemes, culminating in the direct invasion of Ethiopia in October 1935. At the closing hours of the colonial era, Mussolini amassed a fleet of 500 airplanes and a large standing army to invade Ethiopia and wave the flag of the Italian empire in colonial territories in league with other European empires. The 1926 Geneva International agreement that prohibited the use of gases as a weapon of war did not deter Italy, one of its signatories, from spreading the Ethiopian highlands with mustard gas, killing thousands of innocent people and livestock. Further, indiscriminate massacre of Ethiopians regardless of age and gender was the hallmark of the Italian fascist invasion and occupation of Ethiopia.

Mussolini was determined to create an empire for Italy in Africa similar to British and French empires. Ethiopia's successful defense of her sovereignty at the Battle of Adwa in 1896 thwarted the Italian colonial ambition for almost forty years. The 1935 invasion was the belated attempt to fulfill the objectives set at the Berlin Conference. Italy did not heed the culturally and historically deep background of the Ethiopians. Ethiopian national consciousness and pride was ignored. Mussolini paid a heavy price and Ethiopia never completely surrendered. Italy's venture in Ethiopia, according to Sbacchi, was a fiasco. It cost Mussolini not only his life, but more than a billion dollars. Fascism suffered a fatal blow as a result of the failure in Ethiopia.

Mussolini's action had crystallized into the ultimate moral issue at the center of colonialism and empire-building—the issue of self-determination for colonized people everywhere. The brutal aggression against Ethiopia made it clear that the Europeans' intent was to conquer, dominate and exploit all Africans. Mussolini's disregard and outright contempt for the sovereignty of Ethiopia angered and reawakened the African world. A new generation of militant pan-Africanists emerged. They called for decolonization, for elimination of race discrimination in the United States, for African unity and for political empowerment of African people. Mussolini's occupation of Ethiopia was the first stage of Africa's decolonization—and the beginning of a Second World War that led to the defeat of fascism and nazism.

Conclusion

Ethiopia, land of the beginning, has a long and rich history. As the first home of humans, Ethiopia was able to develop the means of human communication that ultimately evolved into numerous languages and knowledge systems. Ethiopia has one of the most advanced and sophisticated writing systems, incorporating elements of pictography, ideography, linguistics, chronology and numerology.

Thousands of years of interactions and economic activity provided the tools for common understanding and national identity in the form of shared values such as language patterns, belief systems, food habits, aesthetic expressions, work habits, and family functions and structures. The solidity of this culture was the root of Adwa's victory and the resistance against fascist aggression.

a halt on the line of march

Even in recent history, thanks to the great accomplishments of leaders such as Tewodros II, Yohannes IV and Menelik II, internal fragmentation and fruitless squabbles were replaced by a centralized state with relations clearly defined between the people and their leaders. Uniform laws were established that united the people as Ethiopians. In other words, national identity in the contemporary sense had already been established and widely accepted for a quarter-century prior to the Battle of Adwa.

Europe conspired to loot and plunder at the 1884–85 Berlin Conference, agreeing on the importance of colonialism for their development. It was at this conference that the Europeans legitimized the genocidal policy of King Leopold II of Belgium by approving his sole possession of the so-called Congo Free State.

Italy as a political state emerged less than 150 years ago when Victor Emanuel II became emperor of the newly established Kingdom of Italy in 1861. The establishment of a unified state set in motion a dynamic process of modernization and colonial expansion. Her aspirations to great power status were partly triggered by the memory of her ancient glorious past. In an attempt to catch up with the European colonial powers, she hastily plunged herself into the "scramble for Africa." The haste became clear when the Ethiopian army defeated the Italian army at the Battle of Adwa in March 1896. Italy became the first European power to be defeated by an African state. As a result, by the end of World War I, Italy had not expanded its colonies very far, confined to "strips of desert in northeast Africa."

Adwa symbolizes the aspirations and hopes of all oppressed people. Adwa catapulted pan-Africanism into the realm of the possible by reigniting the imaginations of Africans in their quest for freedom throughout the world. Adwa foreshadowed the outcome of the anti-colonial struggle. Adwa is about cultural resistance; it is about reaffirmation of African ways. Adwa was possible not simply because of brilliant and courageous leadership but also because of the people's willingness to defend their motherland, regardless of ethnic, linguistic and religious differences. Adwa is a story of common purpose and common destiny. The principles established on the battlefield of Adwa must be understood and embraced for Africa to remain centered in its own histories, cultures and socioeconomic development. We should always remember that Adwa was won for Africans. Adwa indeed is an African model of victory and resistance.

from *Musée Universel*, 1882 *Adwa*

Adwa and Menelik's Ethiopia

Teshale Tibebu

On March 1, 1896 the largest battle between European Imperialism and African resistance took place at Adwa in northern Ethiopia. Led by Emperor Menelik, the Ethiopians with an estimated 100,000 troops defeated a well-armed and well-entrenched Italian army of about 20,000. The Ethiopian victory at the Battle of Adwa sent shockwaves throughout the West. As we observe the centennial of the Battle of Adwa, we should remind ourselves of the world significance of that historic contest. Although Ethiopians might not have seen it that way, the Battle of Adwa and its outcome was seen in the West in racial terms. And, as such, the racially-conscious West saw Adwa as a spoiler of global white supremacy.

Anthony Mockler called the Italian defeat "the greatest single disaster in European colonial history." Akpan, in contrast, saw the outcome of the Battle of Adwa as "the greatest victory of an African over a European army since the time of Hannibal." Dugan and Lafore commented that Adwa not only ensured Ethiopia's survival but also marked the beginning of the end of European global dominance.

Adwa made the West respect Ethiopia and look at Emperor Menelik as a power to be reckoned with. The historic significance of the Battle of Adwa lies not in "black" Africans defeating "white" Europeans, but rather that Ethiopia was recognized as one among the many sovereign states. As to the claim that Adwa was "the greatest victory of an African over a European army since the time of Hannibal," one can recall the January 22, 1879 British defeat by the Zulu at the Battle of Isandhlwana, the defeat of General Gordon at the hands of the Sudanese Ansars, the repeated victory of the Asante over the British and so on, as examples of African military victories over Europeans before Adwa. However, all the pre-Adwa African triumphs were erased from European memory because in each case the victories were temporary.

Thanks to Adwa, the Western image of Ethiopia as a land of "superstition-ridden Christianity" lost in a mountain fastness changed dramatically. In Harold Marcus' words,

> *The Battle of Adwa proved conclusively that an African power could successfully meet the challenge of modern European imperialism: five days [after the battle of Adwa], the Italians recognized the fact by suing for peace. [In the aftermath of Adwa] Europe had to*

reassess Ethiopia and its ruler, in much the same fashion as they would Japan after Russia's defeat in 1905.

As the European scramble for Africa was underway in the last decade of the nineteenth century, there was another scramble taking place in the aftermath of Adwa: the scramble for the recognition of Ethiopian sovereignty. In G.N. Sanderson's words, "Menelik's crushing victory (1 March

Menelik stamp 1894

1896) was followed by intense Anglo-French competition for his goodwill."

To explain the anomaly of the Adwa debacle, the West constructed a new image of Ethiopia and Ethiopians, an image in tune with the racist imperialism of the time—Ethiopians were painted white! If the fact of Ethiopians being black

1908 Nov 1 issue Ethiopian stamp of Menelik in costume

contradicted a racist theory of modern history, then the fact that Ethiopians are black cannot be true. So was born the myth of Ethiopians being "black Caucasians." As Martin Bernal remarked, "Where the racial stereotype of natural European superiority failed, artificial intervention was necessary to preserve it." The "black Caucasian" thesis ascribed to Ethiopians was one such artificial intervention.

As Ethiopians were being painted white, Menelik was being deified as a genius. He was portrayed as industrious, hard-working and disciplined. In the words of the British captain Count Gleichen, who came to Menelik's court in 1897,

> *Were his [Menelik's] subjects but one-tenth part as anxious as himself for civilization and progress, Abyssinia would indeed become a serious factor in the world's game.*[1]

For the American Skinner,

> *Menelik has created the United States of Abyssinia—a work for which he was endowed by Nature with the constructive intelligence of a Bismarck, and the faculty for handling men ... [with the] sheer amiability of a McKinley.*

From an Ethiopian perspective, the Adwa victory gave Ethiopians a sense of pride, indeed, of superiority over the *ferenj* (foreigner). In Gleichen's words:

Up to this time [Adwa] all Europeans had been looked up to in Abyssinia with respect, if not fear. Adwa, to use a vulgarism, upset the apple-cart, and entirely altered the views of the natives. The body of the Abyssinian people even now imagines that their victory has laid not only Italy, but the whole of Europe, at their feet, and their heads are proportionately elevated.

Western racism found Adwa puzzling. Had Adwa been a battle between two European armies, Westerners would have long forgotten it. Was not the South African War (so-called Anglo-Boer War) much more destructive, involving many more troops than Adwa? But then, it was a war between Europeans, and hence not unusual. This was the century of Hegel, Gobineau, Knox and Renan, a century of Western global triumph, a century of Western racism running wild. In this universal triumph of the "rational" West, Adwa came as a spoiler, as an exception to the rule. Better to paint Ethiopians white than to accept the Adwa exception. For the West, the logic was, if you cannot beat them, bleach them. This attitude helps explain how Ethiopians became "honorary whites," as did the Japanese nine years after Adwa when they defeated Mother Russia.

Ethiopians won at Adwa. So were they respected by the West? As Dorothy Hammond and Alta Jablow rightly noted:

Nineteenth-century theories of Social Darwinism, racism, and biological determinism provided justification for the initial conquest and subsequent domination of Africa. According to the tenet of "survival of the fittest," . . . conquest was self-validating. The innate inferiority of the conquered [Africans] was demonstrated by the fact that they were conquered and could be accounted for by their unfitness in the evolutionary contest.[2]

That Ethiopians were superior among Africans, since they won at Adwa, became a popular prejudice in Europe. But when Ethiopians felt superior to Europeans, it was thought absurd. In a racist diatribe, Herbert Vivian, a British traveler in Ethiopia at the end of the nineteenth century, wrote:

It is no doubt reasonable that a nation of niggers, possessing three hundred thousand rifles, should take a tone different from that of niggers who are not permitted to possess any, but they go too far when they presume to arrogate themselves a superiority over civilized countries against which they could not possibly stand up.[3]

For Ethiopians, who had no idea of the hierarchical evaluation of social formations or of stratification by productive achievement that produced material well-being, superiority meant one thing only—victory on the battlefield.

How did Ethiopia (alone, save Liberia) maintain her sovereignty? First, Ethiopia imported more firearms from Europe than any other place in Africa. Second, the history of centuries of statehood—the existence of an armed body separate from the rest of the population, a warrior class (*chawa, watader*), specializing in the art of military science—allowed Ethiopia to escape the European onslaught. Third, the cultural unity established by the Ethiopian Orthodox Church had created a national consciousness of Ethiopia as a "Christian island surrounded by a hostile heathen sea." The Emperor's *negarit* (war drum) sounded the war cry:

ristehen yamiqema haimanotehn yamiarekes mistehen yamidafer telat keruq metobehalena tanasa! Gulbet yaleh bakendeh yalelah batsaloteh takatalegn.

or

ርስትህን የሚቀማ ሀይማኖትህን የሚያረክስ ሚስትህን የሚደፍር ጠላት ከሩቅ ሀገር መጥቶብሀልና ተነሳ ጉልበት ያለህ በጉልበትህ የሌለህ በጸሎትህ ተከተለኝ

An enemy has come from a distant land to take away your land, to destroy your religion, to defy the honor of your wife. Rise up! If you are strong, follow me and render me your arm. If you are weak, pray for my victory.

Land, Religion, Wife—the sacred trinity of Ethiopian "war nationalism"—was worth dying for.

In contrast to the Ethiopian story, state formation in the rest of nineteenth century Africa failed for two primary reasons. First, the states formed were new and fragile (with Egypt as an exception). Second, there was a large military power gap between Europeans and Africans.

◆-◆-◆

Fasil Dawit 1995

Menelik leading his troops into battle

What was the Ethiopian state like, a state that humbled the Italian invaders at Adwa? How could Ethiopia win such a decisive victory? What was the relationship between the army and the people? What kind of army did Ethiopia have? What was its ethnic makeup? The processes of state formation in Ethiopia during the second half of the nineteenth century answers most of these questions. Recent political developments in Ethiopia indicate that it is time for Ethiopians to remember their past.

It has now become commonplace to view Menelik's state as a Shoan Amhara (a single ethnic group) power, magnified by territorial expansion and imperialistic conquest of the Southern peoples of present-day Ethiopia. These polities had an independent life before their conquest and incorporation into Menelik's empire. According to this perspective, the Battle of Adwa is seen as a battle between two imperialist forces—one black, one white—both fighting for Oromo, Gurage, Welaita and other territories. That is, from an Ethiopian perspective, Adwa is viewed as a battle of anti-imperialist imperialism. However, all countries have been built through conquest and consolidation over long periods of time. Ethiopia is no different.

On the contrary, the Battle of Adwa was the most successful multiethnic effort in modern Ethiopian history. Emperor Menelik fought in his capacity as emperor of Ethiopia. Yes, he was from Shoa, and yet he fought in Tigray. If there is doubt about whether Menelik was an Ethiopian—above any ethnic loyalty—Adwa proves it. If one were to read Adwa ethnically, as an Amhara emperor fighting in Tigray against Italians, it would indeed be meaningless. Gojjames, Gondares, Shoans as well as Tigreans, Oromos and Gurages fought side by side against a common threat. Prior to Adwa, Ras Alula stood up at Gundet, Gura and Dogali—not as a Tigrean but as an Ethiopian. So did Emperor Yohannes who mobilized his army in defense of Ethiopia against the Mahdist Ansars. He died at Matamma as an Ethiopian emperor of Ethiopia. The lesson of Adwa is that it is possible, after all, to be supraethnic in identity. It is possible to be Ethiopian.

The beauty of Adwa is that it was a battle of just Ethiopian nationalism standing up against unjust Italian imperialism.

This statement should not, however, make us lose sight of another side of modern Ethiopia: that it expanded its territorial domain under the hegemony of Emperor Menelik, that this expansion has left deep scars on the victims of the expansion, that in order to ensure a healthy future for Ethiopia it is time we examine this scar openly and honestly. The victors of the battle of Adwa are shining stars in the galaxy of Africa's anti-imperialist struggle—and yet, the star of Adwa had also erased other stars of the South, most notably the Oromo star.

◆-◆-◆

How was the modern Ethiopian state formed? It involved three processes: first, centralization of power in the domain of what I call the Ge'ez civilization; second, territorial expansion of the Ge'ez civilization beyond Shoa; and third, collision of interest between Ethiopian rulers and European powers engaged in the scramble for Africa.

Ge'ez civilization state centralization was initiated by *Dejjach* (General) Kassa Hailu who put an end to the power struggle between feudal lords (*Zemena Mesafint* ዘመነ መሳፍንት). After defeating the Tigrean *Dejjach* Wube at the Battle of Darge on February 8, 1855. Kassa Hailu was coronated (Emperor) Atse Tewodros II, supposedly because of a prophecy that a man with his name would reign over Ethiopia and return her to her former, Axumite, glory.

Emperor Tewodros II next defeated and ended the rule of the Yajju Oromo whose capital was Dabra Tabor in the middle of otherwise Amhara lands. In a letter sent to Queen Victoria in 1862, Emperor Tewodros declared:

> *My fathers the Emperors having forgotten our Creator ... handed over their Kingdom to the Gallas and Turks. But God created me, lifted me out of the dust, and restored this Empire to my rule ... By His power I drove away the Gallas [Oromos]. But for the Turks, I have told them to leave the land of my ancestors. They refused. I am going to wrestle with them.*[4]

Oromos had been active participants in the politics of Christian Ethiopia since the time of Emperor Susneyos in the sixteenth century. By the time of the Zemene Mesafint, they were the dominant power brokers. Oromos intermarried with Amharas and left their imprint on Amhara culture—with place names like Basso-Liban and Illmana Densa in Gojjam and Warra Himanu, Warra Illu, Warra Babo in Wello, including the name Wello (ወሎ) itself—and language—with Amharic words such as *dula* (ዱላ, stick), *chafe* (ጨፌ, marshland), *chifra* (ጭፍራ, troops) and so on.

Although Tewodros initiated the centralization of state power, it was the Tigrean emperor Yohannes IV who "imagined" modern Ethiopia with well-defined territorial boundaries. In a letter written to Kaiser Wilhelm I, King of Prussia, dated February 17, 1881 Emperor Yohannes IV said:

> *To the east and the south[east] the boundary is the sea. To the west and north, where there are not seas, it is bounded by Nuba, Suakin, Khartoum, Berber, Sennar, Ennaria, Sudan, and then Dongola, Haren Dawa, Gash, Massawa, Bedun, Shoho, and Tiltal. Further, the regions inhabited by Galla, Shankilla, and Adal is [sic] all mine, and yet recently in the middle of Shoa, a place known by the name Harar, was taken [from us]. All the same I listed these places so that my country's boundaries be known.*[5]

So while Emperor Tewodros II initiated and Emperor Yohannes IV elaborated, Emperor Menelik II consolidated and Emperor Haile Selassie I completed the process of modern Ethiopian statehood.

Modern state formation in Ethiopia, as elsewhere, meant

- territorial expansion and integration;
- bringing previously autonomous and semiautonomous polities under centralized authority;
- predominance of the role of the army in the initial process of state formation;
- a more or less defined boundary;
- an elaborate system of taxation; and
- membership in the interstate system.

African leaders like emperors Tewodros II and Menelik II—as well as Samori Toure of West Africa, Shaka of Zulu Kingdom, Mutesa of Uganda, etc.—recognized the critical role the army plays in state formation and consolidation. Moreover, states formed in nineteenth century Ethiopia, as elsewhere in Africa, took place in conflict with European expansion. For this, the acquisition of firearms was simply indispensable.

The role of firearms in the making of modern Ethiopia can be seen from two angles. From within, superior firepower and the locale that harbored this firepower asserted its dominance over the area. Shoa was that locale. Geographically speaking, the center, Shoa, was dominant over both the north (the hitherto dominant locale of arms superiority) and the south. Externally, Ethiopian firearms enabled the Adwa victory.

The critical role of firearms in state formation was well understood by Europeans. As Hilaire Belloc put it:

Whatever happens we have got
The maxim–gun and they have not.

Modern Ethiopia was born of the defeat of the peoples of southern regions as well as Egypt and Italy. As elsewhere in state formations, the "end"—unity of modern Ethiopia—came through the "means"—brutality. With its victory over Muslim Egypt, Catholic Italy and "pagan" and Muslim south, Ethiopia entered the era of its modern history.

It is a mistake to draw (the sometimes commonplace) analogy between Menelik's expansion and European colonialism in Africa since race was not involved with the southern peoples. Negus Mikael of Wallo, Empress Mennen (Haile Selassie's wife), Haile Selassie's grandfather Wolde Mikael Gudissa, Lidj Eyasu, the Wellega notables who joined the royal family through marriage, were all Oromos. The ruler/ruled divide in southern Ethiopia was a cultural/class divide, not a racial one. It could be crossed over, but only through a one-way assimilation process into the Ge'ez civilization. Marriage into the ruling group was one way of doing so. Imagine a Zulu "paramount chief" joining Buckingham Palace in holy matrimony!

For the conquered peoples of the south, Amhara meant "one with power," and the person identified as such could be an Oromo from Shoa, a Gurage, a Tigrean, an Eritrean or an Amhara. For Muslims and followers of "traditional" African religions, Amhara meant "Christian with a gun."

Adwa is an African victory over European imperialism. Adwa is a victory over racism. Adwa is a victory over ethnocentrism. Adwa is the jewel and pride of Africa. Let us celebrate its centennial. May Adwa guide us in the spirit of reconciliation, ethnic harmony and dedication to maintaining Ethiopia's sovereignty.

Symbol of Freedom

Fikre Tolossa

"Give me guns, soldiers and money,"
bragged General Baratieri with monotony,
"and I'll bring you Menelik in a cage
to make him the laughingstock of the age
and for all Europe to see that he's savage,
and to teach the uncivilized black man
that no black man whatsoever can
beat up the great white man!
I'll bring you slaves, gold and ivory, oh, Rome!
Oh, Romans! Ethiopia will be your second home
I'll make you great, and set your hearts afire
as in the days when you ruled the Roman Empire!"

"I'll divide those Africans by tribe
I'll give each leader a bribe
and rule them while they fight each other
isolating Menelik, so that he can't gather
the different tribes to fight beloved Italy
and thus defeat and capture him easily!"

So boasting General Baratieri made a cage
to make Menelik the laughingstock of the age.

Italy's emperor, the pope and the people,
the scholar and the layman, the able and cripple,
supported Baratieri in euphoria to dominate
old Ethiopia, her army to exterminate
so that she will never rise from her fall
and to enslave her children once and for all.

"Get now ready, Menelik," said Empress
Taitu to her husband to encourage and to press
him to fight bravely the brutal enemy
trusting God, raising a mighty army.

Said Menelik, "Let's give peace a chance
let's settle our differences once
again, let's negotiate before we spill
the blood of fellow humans, before we do ill."

"What ill! What spilling of blood," she spoke
"What humanitarians! What a joke!
Save your country Menelik, arise! fight!
Defend your honor with God's might!"

Persuaded to fight by his brave wife
Menelik answered the call of his life.

"Hear ye my people! hear ye my people!
Man, woman, young, old, noble or simple
defend your motherland, arise and fight
lest you're raped and shackled in a merciless blight
they contemptuously call us savage and pagans
to plunder Africa and enslave us Africans!"

The Oromo, Amhara, Tigre, Afar, Somali, Gurage, Hadia
the Adere, Welaita, all the children of Ethiopia
responding to his call, gathered around their emperor
like bees around their queen, displaying terror
scaring their enemy with their unbreakable unity
their love for their country, their bond and affinity.

In eighteen ninety-six, the year of great fears
Italy's mortars thundered, Menelik fought with spears,
swords and guns that were hardly firing
whereas Italy's countless weapons were awe-inspiring.

Menelik's generals fought heroically, nobody fled
from the battlefield, unlike the Italians led
by General Baratieri, the first to flee like a rabbit
throwing away his gun cowardly, running in orbit
his hat and pants falling off in shame
enraging the whole of Rome, disgracing his name
scattering the corps of his soldiers and generals behind
forgetting about them, bearing his safety in mind
abandoning the wounded and the sick in the sands
leaving the captives in Menelik's hands.

Empress Taitu the bright, Ethiopia's sunlight
gathered her own army, ready for a fight
nursing the wounded, encouraging the hesitant
rewarding the brave at each and every instant.

Now the name Menelik became a song sung
among those subdued in Asia and among
those trampled over in Africa
Latin America and Jamaica
the name Ethiopia became the symbol of freedom
a pride for blacks of the earth, a mighty kingdom.
The Caesar of Rome and his subjects could no more boast.
and brag about their greatness anymore from one coast
of Italy to another, as they did previously
since they were beaten up, obviously.

Who beat them? Ethiopians who built obelisks and towers
and ate from plates of gold, counted among the major powers
of the world, when yet the children without mother or home
Remus and Romulus the builder of Rome
were being suckled by a she-wolf in a hole
leading the life of animals, such as the mole.

Thousands and thousands wounded or killed
with their blood and corps the fields were filled
after the war and Italy's defeat
angry mobs took over Italy's streets
to tear down the parliament and with a great rage
to take Prime Minister Crispi and his cliques hostage.
"Viva! Menelik, our hero, the one and only,"
cried the mob, "come lead us, come rule Italy!
Be gone, Emperor Umberto! Menelik is our king!
In praise of Menelik, let our women sing!
She who has charmed Europe, let Taitu be our queen
a woman as tough as her, who has ever seen?"

sick and wounded Italian soldiers from Massowa being taken into the hospital

Mothers and grandmothers flooded the capital,
with anguish and sorrow some landed in hospital
inquiring about their children, begging the pope
to appeal to Menelik, not losing hope,
that kind Menelik would forgive the crime
of their sons, so that they could enjoy the prime
of their life returning home. The pope likewise,
sent a letter to Menelik, calling him wise,
merciful ruler, benevolent and magnanimous,
every inch emperor, illustrious and famous.

Elsewhere in London, Paris, Berlin and Madrid
there was turmoil, everyone asking the question, "How did
poorly armed Africans defeat Europeans?"
And they all considered it a bad omen.

When those surviving Italians later came near
Menelik, they were ashamed and shivered in fear
But he, a kind-hearted, magnanimous emperor
was grief stricken instead of showing wrath and anger.
Looking at those who were collapsing, unable to stand,
he said, "Sorry for you, though you came to take our land."

Turning to his soldiers, he said, "Show clemency!
Why kill your captives who are at your mercy?
Offer them food and water abundantly, go get
them clothes and shoes, and don't forget
to give each of them an allowance in accordance
with his rank, now do what I said, at once!"
When Menelik let the prisoners go to their country
for their mother's sake, they said, "We're sorry
for fighting you unjustly, our erroneous plan was simple—
it was to colonize and civilize your people
But who's to civilize who in reality?
you've civilized us and taught us morality."

Thus Menelik and his people, the Oromo, Amhara, Tigre,
the Welaita, Afar, Somali, Gurage and Adere
fought ferociously to keep their beloved country
forever free from the shackles of slavery,
lighting the torch of freedom, setting example
to all the world's colonized and oppressed people.

October 19, 1995

Menelik's Proclamation on Mobilizing His Forces for The Battle of Adwa

God by his goodness in hurling down my enemies and extending my empire has preserved me until this day. Until now I have ruled by the grace of God. As we all must die I shall not be distressed if I am killed. Nevertheless the Almighty has never yet forsaken me and I am confident that he will not forsake me in the future.

Enemies have now come upon us to ruin the country and to change our religion; they have crossed the sea which God has given us for a frontier. Considering that our flocks were exterminated and our people tired, I have not wished to do anything until now.

But our enemies have begun the affair by advancing and digging into the country like moles. With the help of God I will not deliver up my country to them. Ever a patriot of my country I have never yet wronged you and I will never give you sorrow. To-day, you who are strong, give me of your strength, and you who are weak, help me by prayer and by thinking of your children, your wives and your faith. But if through negligence you refuse to follow me, take heed. You will hate me because I will not refrain from punishing you. I swear by the Holy Virgin that I will accept no prayer for your pardon. I leave in the month of Teqemt. Men of Shoa, go and wait for me at Warra Ilu; let everyone be assembled by the middle of Teqemt!

አዋጅ

እግዚአብሔር በቸርነቱ እስካሁን ጠላት አጥፍቶ አገር አስፍቶ አኖረኝ። እኔም እስካሁን በእግዚአብሔር ቸርነት ገዛሁ።

እንግዲህ ብሞትም ሞት የሁሉ ነውና ስለኔ ሞት አላዝንም። ደግሞ እግዚአብሔር አሳፍሮኝ አያውቅም ወደፊትም ያሳፍረኛል ብዬ አልጠራጠርም።

አሁንም አገር የሚያጠፋ ሃይማኖት የሚለውጥ ጠላት እግዚአብሔር የወሰነልንን ባህር አልፎ መጥቷል።

እኔም ያገሬን ከብት ማለቅ የሰውን መድከም አይቼ እስካሁን ዝም ብለው ደግሞ እያለፈ እንደፍልፈል መሬት ይቆፍር ጀመር።

አሁን ግን በእግዚአብሔር ረዳትነት አገሬን አሳልፌ አልሰጠውም። ያገሬ ሰው ካሁን ቀደም የበደልሁህ አይመስለኝም። አንተም እስካሁን አላስቀየምኸኝም።

ጉልበት ያለህ በጉልበትህ እርዳኝ። ጉልበት የሌለህ ለልጅህም ለምሽትህም ለሃይማኖትህ ስትል በሐዘን እርዳኝ። ወስልተህ የቀረህ ግን፡ ኋላ ትጣላኛለህ አልተውህም ማርያምን ለዚህ አማላጅ የለኝም።

ዘመቻዬ፡ በጥቅምት ነውና የሸዋ ሰው እስከ ጥቅምት እኩሌታ ድረስ ወረይሉ ከተህ ላግኝህ።

Empress Taitu from J. Borelli, *Ethiopie méridionale*, Paris 1890

from J. Borelli, *Ethiopie méridionale*, Paris 1890

Emperor Menelik II

Italian soldiers watching Ethiopian troops draw near

Fasil Dawit 1995

The Battle

Richard Pankhurst

The campaign of Adwa began between January 24 and 30, 1896 when Emperor Menelik, taking advantage of Ras Makonnen's victories at Amba Alagi and Makelle, marched onward to Hausen and then to Adwa. This advance outmaneuvered the Italian commander General Baratieri by disrupting communications with his base at Asmara. Accordingly, on February 1, Baratieri moved back the bulk of his army from Edagahamus to Mai Gabeta—and two days later concentrated his forces between Mai Gabeta and Entichio. Menelik's armies had meanwhile taken up positions on the hills northeast of Adwa, only five miles away. The two armies, which had once opposed each other looking north and south, thus faced east and west and were close enough to open hostilities.

The Italians, however, were finding communications difficult. The country was so mountainous that transport animals moved slowly and had often to climb dangerous precipices, made even more dangerous by hostile forces behind them. And, due to a recent epidemic, only about 20 percent of the local mules were fit for service. The Italians had been relying on two local chiefs, Ras Sebhat and Ras Agas Tafari, who knew the country well, to help guide them. But they had recently come out in support of Menelik.

Finally, Italian morale disintegrated. Baratieri and his staff quarreled about strategy while all sorts of rumors circulated among the officers and men. It was said that agents from the Ethiopian side freely entered the Italian camp; while the Italians, who could not count on the support of the local population, often used spies. These spies were, in fact, on Menelik's side. Baratieri was the only person who believed their reports. Moreover, Italian field maps were completely inaccurate.

Baratieri's plan was to remain entrenched in his position and wait there in the hope that Menelik would attack—or be forced to fall back due to a lack of provisions. Although the Ethiopians could marshal very large forces, they had no transport to bring up supplies from the rear. The huge army and its hordes of camp followers and servants depended on what they could procure locally. If this source failed they had to march into other areas. Further, Baratieri was determined not to move both supplies and men because of the dangerous terrain and his personal unpopularity in the area. A.B. Wylde observes that Baratieri had "a very bad name in Adwa, owing to the cruelties that took place when he first occupied the town."

Menelik, who took up his final position at Adwa on January 21, was also determined to wait for his opponent to make the first move. On January 23 he ordered Ras Mangesha, Ras Makonnen, Fitawrari Gabiehu, Fitawrari Tekle and Likemekusas Adanou to march northward to Addi Koula, where they were to await his arrival. But a shortage of water obliged Menelik's force to return to base. On the following day, January 24, the Italians attempted an attack but as soon as the Ethiopians indicated that they were ready to retaliate, the Italians returned to their fort, much to the discontent of Menelik and his men. The Ethiopians complained that the enemy was like a tortoise that retreated into its shell whenever approached. According to Gabre Selassie's *Chronicle of the Reign of Menilek*, the emperor was provoked into ordering an attack until reminded of the losses incurred by the Emperor Yohannes in the assault of Metemma. Menelik therefore decided not to move until the invader launched an attack.

Consequently, says Gabre Selassie, the Ethiopian command decided, after long discussions on February 26 and 27, not to attack unless the Italians themselves began operations. If there was no sign of enemy movement and their own men then searching for forage arrived in time, the army would proceed into Hamasien, probably on March 2. Such a move would offer another opportunity to threaten Italian lines of communication. But it was destined never to be.

Meanwhile, indecision reigned in the Italian camp. Though well entrenched, Baratieri was increasingly preoccupied with transport difficulties. To make matters worse, on February 25 he received Prime Minister Crispi's fateful telegram. It informed him that his government, for political reasons, insisted on a victory and was "ready for any sacrifice." On February 28 Baratieri ordered his army to move back, as his position seemed to him unsatisfactory. It was the third time the hesitating commander had given the order to retreat. General Dabormida, doubtless having in mind Crispi's telegram, spoke for all when he said, "Italy would prefer the loss of two or three thousand men to a retreat which would seem dishonorable." Finally, on February 29, Baratieri gave the decisive command to attack.

According to Ethiopian tradition Baratieri made the decision to attack because he had received intelligence reports that Menelik was in no position to resist. It is asserted that a certain Awalom, a villager of Entichio, had some time earlier made contact with the Italians by supplying them with eggs, chickens and other produce and had been given $200 by Baratieri to undertake espionage work. Awalom, described as a tall man of soldierly bearing, was entirely loyal to the Ethiopian cause and went immediately to Ras Mangesha to report the confidence placed in him by the invader. It is related that Mangesha interrogated him privately and, convinced of the truth of his story, disguised him as one of his own guards to avoid drawing attention to the matter. He then took him to Menelik and his generals. Ras Alula, who was present, urged Awalom to give false information to the enemy. Menelik agreed and gave Awalom a sum of money. Instead, Awalom offered the emperor the $200 he had received from the Italians as his own personal contribution to the war. Menelik laughingly refused to accept the money and asked the patriot to follow through with Alula's plan. Awalom reluctantly agreed, because he had hoped to join Menelik's armies as a soldier.

Awalom returned to Baratieri's camp where he is said to have told the Italian commander that it was necessary to attack at once as the Ethiopian army was scattered in search of food. The latter statement was, of course, true and was confirmed by Baratieri's spies. The writings of A.B. Wylde also corroborate this account. Asserting that Entichio was the wrong base for an attack on Adwa, Wylde declares,

> *I have every reason to know that the (Italian) Intelligence Department was altogether at fault regarding the actual number of Abyssinian soldiers present and did not give them the credit for having the number of rifles or the quantity of ammunition they possessed.*

Awalom, it is related, acted as guide to part of the Italian army and led them toward the armies of Ras Mangesha and Ras Alula. He then escaped the invading army and joined the Ethiopian forces so that he could take part in the battle. He was later appointed the *Chika-Shum* of his village and given exemption from paying taxes. During the Italian occupation, which began forty years later, some of his relatives fled to

Shire to avoid the invader's wrath; others were exiled to Nakura.

Baratieri's new plan was to advance by night in three columns, each made up of one brigade, with a fourth brigade following as a reserve in the rear. The objective was to occupy positions some nine miles ahead and only four miles from the Ethiopians who, he hoped, would be obliged by this maneuver either to retreat or to retaliate. A.B. Wylde comments:

> *General Baratieri thought his attack would have been a complete surprise, and as Signor Crispi, the Prime Minister, wanted to meet his Parliament (which was discontented with the policy in Eritrea) with a victory, no reward for General Baratieri would have been too great had he succeeded, and, like a gamester, he threw his dice for a big coup and lost.*

The country to be crossed was extremely rough and the population hostile. An Italian officer, describing the physical features of the land, referred to the

> *rugged slopes, precipitous and broken, abounding in ravines, gorges and crevasses; narrow and tortuous clefts in the hard rock; passes half-closed, steep and very difficult, and granite summits that rear themselves to the sky in the most strange forms and dimensions. The surface seemed like a stormy sea moved by the anger of God.*

The Italian force numbered 20,000 well-equipped men and 56 cannon, according to G.F.H. Berkeley in *The Campaign of Adowa and the Rise of Menelik*. This force, 17,700 strong (10,596 Italian, the remainder Eritrean)—took part in the operation while 1,466 Italians and 1,600 Eritreans were left behind in the camp.

The Ethiopians, on the other hand, were considerably more numerous, but less well equipped. It is estimated that they had about 80,000 riflemen, 8,600 cavalry, 20,000 spearmen and 42 cannon. According to Melli, these forces were divided among the principal Ethiopian commanders listed below.

The Ethiopian rifles were mainly breech-loaders obtained from French, Belgian, Russian and other sources. The Ethiopian cannon were mainly obsolete models, though they included a number of Hotchkiss guns that, according to A.B. Wylde, were

	Rifles	Horses	Guns
Emperor Menelik	25,000	3,000	32
Empress Taitu	3,000	600	4
King Tekla Haimanot	5,000		
Ras Makonnen	15,000		
Ras Mangesha and Alula	12,000		
Ras Mangesha Atichim	6,000		6
Ras Mikael	6,000	5,000	
Ras Olie	8,000		
Totals:	**80,000**	**8,600**	**42**

superior to anything the Italians possessed and were to prove of great value. However, the Italians made no use of cavalry, despite knowing that the British had found them most useful during the Magdala campaign of 1867–68. Nor did they use heliographs (mirrors for sending messages) during the battle, though these were also available.

Ras Makonnen and his Harari forces occupied Adwa itself and the heights above it. To the right, south of the city on a high irregular plateau with its flanks protected by nearly perpendicular cliffs, up which there were only a few sheep paths, lay the troops of King Tekla Haimanot. His cavalry extended out at the foot of the cliffs among the meadows. On the left wing lay Ras Mikael with his Oromo cavalry along the southern and southwestern slopes of Mount Selado. Adjoining him on the mountain's north and northwest sides were Ras Mangesha and his Tigrean troops; while on the extreme left, as far back as the heights of Adi Abuna, lay the forces of Ras Alula. Menelik and Empress Taitu made up the rear. Stationed near the ruins of the Jesuit monastery at Fremona, they were encamped on rocky ground that offered great opportunities for stubborn resistance, while at the same time within easy access of the rest of the army. If needed, they could easily move up in support of Ras Alula, Ras Makonnen or Ras Mikael. Ras Wole was encamped on low ground to the southwest of the Fremona spur, immediately behind Ras Makonnen, whom he could reinforce in less than half an hour, while Wagshum Guangul lay behind Ras Makonnen and King Tekla Haimanot, either of whom he could join if needed. The Oromo cavalry was encamped in meadows eight miles away.

The Italian advance began by the light of the moon at 9:00 P.M. on February 29. Smoking was prohibited so that the troop movement would not be observed by the unsuspecting Ethiopians. Dabormida's brigade was on the right, Arimondi's in the center and Albertone's on the left. Ellena, with the reserve brigade, followed Arimondi. From the outset, however, Baratieri found it impossible to keep the three lines abreast. Perhaps led astray by faulty intelligence, he was himself slow to take up a central position in the Memsah valley and failed to place Ellena's reserves in a position where they could support either the flanks or the center.

At about 2:30 A.M. on March 1, Albertone's brigade crossed Arimondi's, causing a one-and-a-half-hour delay. At 3:00 A.M. he reached the hill (named Kidane Meheret on Baratieri's map, though not generally known by that name) he had been ordered to occupy to make contact with Arimondi. Not realizing that he had delayed the latter, Albertone waited impatiently for half an hour. Thinking there was some mistake about the location, he consulted his guides and was told that Kidane Meheret was some four and a half miles further from Sauria.

After another half hour's wait, Albertone set off at full pace in the hope of making up for lost time in the direction of the true Kidane Meheret that overlooked Adwa and was just three miles from Menelik's camp. There he found himself isolated and surrounded by Ethiopian troops, compelling the other brigades to fight all day with their left flank unguarded. Within two and a half miles of his new objective he halted in an effort to make contact with the force he believed to be on his right. The advance guard failed to receive his order, however, and continued to march—with the result that at 6:00 A.M. he found himself engaged alone in fierce combat.

Meanwhile, the other units were moving according to plan. Baratieri himself reached Rebbi Arienni at 6:00 A.M.. Hearing some distant firing, he assumed it was the advance guard and that Albertone was in his allotted position. Dabormida had reached a position not far from his commander. Arimondi had moved up the eastern slopes of the same high land. In the rear Ellena's reserve column came into sight. All seemed well, except that Albertone's conscripts had taken a wrong path and were nowhere to be seen.

General Baratieri

The Italians had been counting on taking the Ethiopians by surprise. Baratieri had only just sent a letter discussing peace terms and expected that hostilities would be deferred until a reply had been returned by Menelik or Ras Makonnen, who had been in charge of negotiations with the enemy. A.B. Wylde declares that "a sort of armistice" therefore existed and that the Italian trick was "what we should call very bad form, and

Empress Taitu inspires her troops: "Courage!" Fasil Dawit 1995

perhaps by a much harsher term." As soon as Baratieri moved, Wylde continues,

> *two of (Ras Alula's) spies watched the Italians leave Entichio and arrived by a circuitous route and informed Ras Alula. The Ras immediately informed King Menelik and the other leaders.*

A large number of Ethiopian soldiers who had gone to the sacred city of Aksum for a religious ceremony celebrated on that day had no intimation of the battle until the boom of cannon, echoing from hill to hill, summoned them. Gabre Selassie, on the other hand, who makes no reference to the role of Awalom, relates the events somewhat differently.

Just before dawn Ras Mangesha's soldiers captured two men who, on being interrogated, revealed that

> *... the Italians, knowing that a large part of Menelik's army have left to obtain provisions, and that the camp is almost empty, have decided to fall upon you by surprise.*

According to Gabre Selassie, Menelik was first warned of the surprise attack by Kagnazmatch Tafessa.

"Do you really believe the enemy is going to attack and that this is not merely another trick to force me again to rally uselessly for battle?" asked the Emperor.

"Today it is certain." Tafessa replied.

Orders were immediately given to prepare for battle. But it was not, says A.B. Wylde, until between 9:00 and 10:00 P.M. that the main Ethiopian force could be brought into action. Two-thirds of the army, Gabre Selassie confirms, were not in the camp; part were foraging for food and part were attending a service at the Church of Mariam Sion.

The first exchange of shots took place about 6:00 A.M. when, as we have seen, Albertone's isolated force found itself in conflict with Ethiopian troops. The chronicler adds that their noise "resembled the rain of Hamle, which falls without stopping." At 6:45 A.M., Dabormida was ordered to occupy the spur of Belah which was more or less in the direction of the gunfire. This advance would have supported Albertone—if he had in fact been where he was assumed to be. Unfortunately for Dabormida, instead of inclining to the left he inclined to the right. Thus, rather than getting closer to the missing general, he continued parallel to him. Consequently, there was a two and a half mile gap of mountainous country between them that the Ethiopians promptly occupied.

Meanwhile, Baratieri, stationed on Rebbi Arienni, was giving orders as though his forces were stationed in the positions he had ordered. At 8:15 A.M. he took a stand on Mount Eshaho, and to his surprise saw that Albertone was seriously engaged. At 9:00 A.M., however, he received two notes from Albertone written at 7:30 and 8:15 A.M. stating that all was more or less well but that reinforcements would be acceptable. The commander promptly galloped to Mount Rajo where he saw to his dismay a routed army streaming back from Mount Rajo to Sauria. He sent officers in vain to stem the rout. "The Ethiopians," declared Major Gammera, an eyewitness, had "maneuvered with great skill" and finally charged with "a hurricane of 25,000 men." The Italians fought back, "but cold, inexorable as death, a storm of lead arrested them."

On the Ethiopian side morale was high. Empress Taitu, in particular, showed great fortitude and, in the words of the chronicler, "ceased to be a mere woman and appeared as a valiant soldier." When she saw the troops waver she cried out "Courage, the victory is ours! Forward!"

Baratieri, though now fully aware of his grave position, was still completely ignorant of the true state of affairs, as he had no contact with units beyond his own immediate vicinity. At 9:15 A.M. he sent a note to Dabormida ordering him to cover Albertone's retirement. The note was not delivered. The messenger met another messenger from Dabormida bringing word that "he was holding out his hand to Albertone" and therefore thought it was useless to deliver the order.

At 9:30 A.M. Baratieri ordered Albertone to retreat, but the messenger failed to arrive safely and eventually learned that Albertone had been killed and that his army was in full retreat. At 9:45 A.M. he sent a messenger to locate Dabormida, but only received confused intelligence reports that turned out to be altogether incorrect. At 10:00 A.M. and again at 10:15 A.M., he sent orders to Dabormida to move forward to support Albertone, but Dabormida was not to be found. He had already begun an advance that would take him into the Mariam Shavita valley, where he was killed.

Baratieri now reinforced his left flank in the belief that the spur of Belah, upon which everything depended, was still held by Dabormida. In fact, it was no longer occupied by any troops

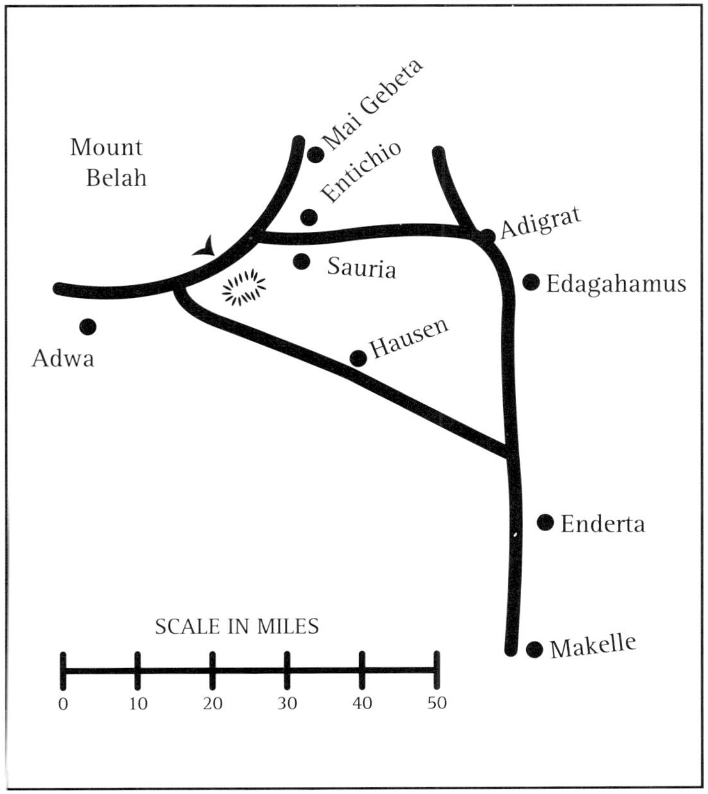

January 24–February 29: maneuvers before the battle

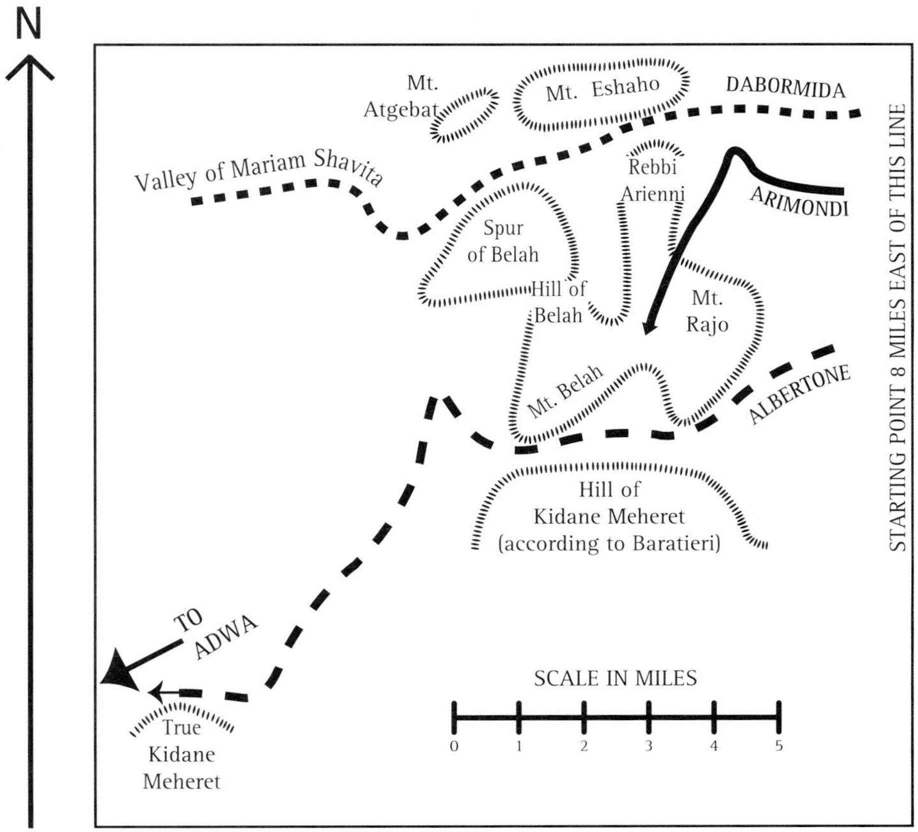

March 1, 1896: the battle

at all. Dabormida was by now four miles to the west. Consequently Ethiopian forces poured in, sweeping past Arimondi's right and cutting his line of retreat. The Ethiopians pursued the routed Italians and, moreover, were able to penetrate within rifle range as the Italians were unable to fire on them for fear of hitting their own stragglers.

The victorious Ethiopians south of Mount Belah now attacked Arimondi's central forces. Galliano brought his Eritrean (Askaris) troops up from reserve to the southern slopes of Mount Rajo. At about 10:15 A.M., another Ethiopian force swept over the hill and spur of Belah from the east, thereby cutting off Baratieri completely from Dabormida and threatening Arimondi, this time from the right. Fifteen minutes later Galliano's Eritrean force deserted to the Ethiopians, enabling Menelik's forces to sweep forward in that sector, thus almost completely surrounding the Italians.

Since both his flanks were now turned, Baratieri determined on a general retreat, which he hoped to effect under cover of Dabormida's force, then fighting hopelessly in the Mariam Shavita valley. By this time, however, complete confusion reigned in the Italian army.

The retreat inexorably turned into a rout as repeated efforts to hold the Ethiopian forces proved hopeless. Italian morale collapsed as the exhausted troops struggled back. Baratieri states:

> *They were almost unconscious of their surroundings, and careless of everything except their individual defense. The officers had lost authority over the soldiers, who looked in a bewildered and stupefied manner at those who gave an order or attempted to halt them.*

The flight continued into the dark. The Ethiopians pursued their foes as far as the River Mareb. During the night many Italians, including the commander himself, lost their way. Declared Baratieri:

> *A terrible destiny weighed on my head; it was the third time that I had lost my way during the retreat, and my heart was breaking at the long hours during which it had been impossible to give my orders or to receive information.*

◆-◆-◆

In chronicling this series of mistakes and mishaps one is entitled to wonder what would have been the course of events if the Italians had employed other tactics. A.B. Wylde offers the following reply:

> *The opinion of Ras Alula and many of the Abyssinian generals was that it made very little difference what took place the moment the Italians made their fatal advance, and if they had made the surprise complete and lined the position, they would still have been beaten and crushed ... I perfectly agree with their opinion, and the loss to both sides would then have been too terrible to contemplate.*

As the survivors of the defeated army retreated across the Eritrean frontier panic spread among the entire Italian population. Italian agricultural colonists abandoned their recently acquired lands and fled to Asmara, and then to port at Massawa. Remnants of the army found their way to the fortresses of Adi Ugrim Asmara, Adi Caieh and the Hadras pass.

On March 6 Baratieri learned that even before the battle the Italian government had decided upon his dismissal. Accordingly, on that day, he handed over control to his successor, Baldissera.

For a week or so it appeared that Menelik would follow up his victory by advancing into Eritrea. On March 12 he encamped at Feres Mai, an advanced post that seemed to indicate an intention of moving on Gura. On March 20, however, to the great relief of the Italians, he ordered his troops to return southward. Afterward, to a priest of Serae (on the way to Gura), he is reported to have said:

> *We were very near to your country and intended to go there. I was not able to do so—first of all because we were short of water; and secondly, because many new enemies had arrived, and, as you know, I do not love spilling blood.*

"The only thing that prevented King Menelik from following up his complete victory," confirms A.B. Wylde, "was want of provisions to feed his army."

Had Ras Alula been allowed to advance with his forces, strengthened by part of Ras Mangesha's force, "there is not doubt," adds A.B. Wylde,

> *the whole of the Hamasien plateau and the Bogos province, with the exception of the fortified positions of Adi Ugri, Asmara and Keren, would have again fallen into the hands of the Abyssinians ... the garrisons of these places were not numerous enough to take the offensive in the open and it would only have been a question of time how long their provisions held out before they would have to capitulate, as it was hardly possible for reinforcements to have arrived from Italy in time to relieve them. The Italian force, immediately after the battle, was a great deal too demoralized to offer any effective resistance.*

At the battle of Adwa, the Italians lost, according to their own figures, the following: 2,918 Italian troops killed, 954 missing, 470 wounded and 1,865 prisoners taken, as well as 2,261 Askaris killed and 958 wounded. These losses represented a large proportion of the total force of 10,598 Italians and 7,100 Askaris. The debacle was however far greater than the figures suggest, because the survivors were completely demoralized. Three major generals who had taken part in the campaign—Albertone, Arimondi and Dabormida—were killed. Baratieri's army had ceased to exist as a fighting unit. Among the booty was the entire Italian artillery, some 65 cannon, 11,000 rifles and most of the transport. The Ethiopians had lost 5,000 to 6,000 men and 8,000 were badly wounded. Among the dead were Kegnazmatch Abaynah, Kegnazmatch Tafessa, Dejazmatch Chacha, Fitawraris Gabiehu, Damtaw, and Dejazmatch Basha Aboye, who died of his wounds on the following day.

Battle Chronology

1/23	*Italians* make show of attacking, but retreat to fort when Ethiopians move to give battle
1/24-30	*Emperor Menelik* marches to Adwa and cuts Baratieri off from Asmara base
2/1-3	*Baratieri* moves army from Edagahamus to between Mai Gabeta and Entichio
2/3	*Menelik*'s armies reposition to east of Italians
2/25	*Baratieri* receives Prime Minister Crispi's telegram insisting on victory at "any sacrifice"
2/26-7	*Ethiopian Command* decides not to attack but to cut off Italians by moving to Hamasien March 2
2/28	*Baratieri* orders army to move back
2/29	*Dabormida* pressures Baratieri to attack
2/29	*Awalom* becomes double-agent; urges Baratieri to attack Ethiopians, busy gathering food
9:00 P.M.	Italian advance begins with three flanks: *Dabormida* on the right *Arimondi* in the center *Albertone* on the left *Ellena* in reserve
3/1	
2:30 A.M.	*Arimondi's* flank delayed $1^1/2$ hours by Albertone
3:00	*Arimondi* reaches what he thinks is Kidane Meheret, but isn't, and waits 1 hour
4:00	*Arimondi* sets off for real Kidane Meheret overlooking Adwa 3 miles from Menelik's camp
6:00	*Armondi* is surrounded by Ethiopian troops before reaching Kidane Meheret
	Baratieri reaches Rebbi Arienni, hears firing *Dabormida* arrives in position *Ellena* arrives in position *Albertone* becomes seriously engaged

8:15 *Baratieri* takes stand on Mount Eshaho, sees *Albertone* in trouble

9:00 *Baratieri* receives notes from *Albertone* requesting reinforcements; goes to look from Mount Rajo and sees Albertone's troops retreating

9:15 *Baratieri* sends to *Dabormida* to cover Albertone's retreat. Note isn't delivered when messenger intercepts Dabormida's request for Albertone's help

9:30 Messenger finds out *Albertone* killed

9:45 *Baratieri* sends messages to *Dabormida* but can't find him

Dabormida killed in Mariam Shavita Valley

Ethiopians follow Arimondi's retreat and overpower them

10:15 *Ethiopians* cut off Baratieri from Dabormida and threaten Armondi forces

10:30 *Galliano's* Eritrean troops desert to the Ethiopians; forces completely surrounded

3/12 *Menelik* encamps at Feres Mai, advancing toward Eritrea

3/20 *Menelik* orders his troops to retire southward

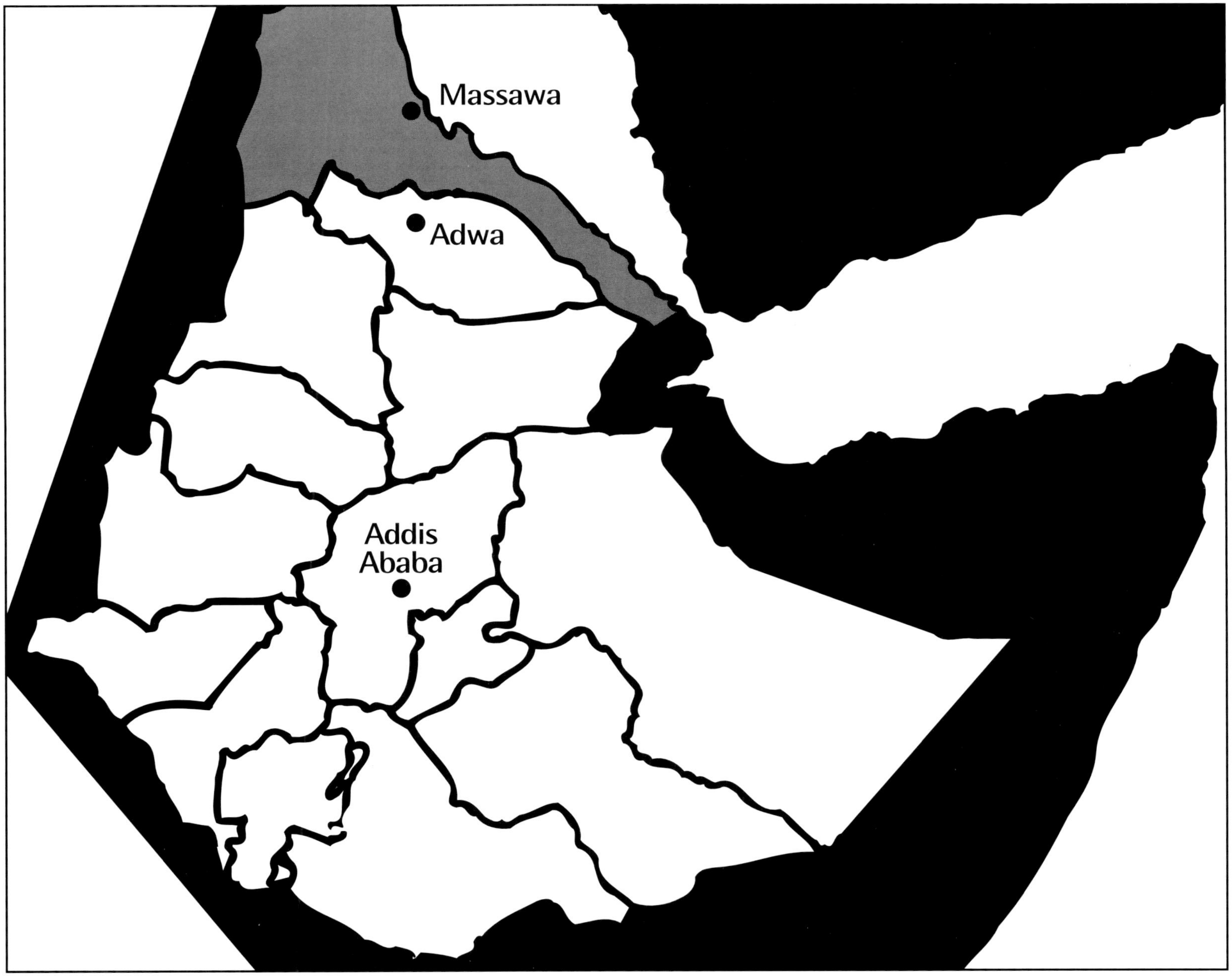

Map of Ethiopia

late 19th century Oromo shield, like those used at the Battle of Adwa

Mingei International Museum of World Folk Art
San Diego, California, USA

acquired by Lucy Bentinck, wife of Sir Charles Bentinck,
Minister in Addis Ababa from 1925–1929

Royal Asiatic Society
London, England

the Battle of Adwa, c.1925
Menelik and Taitu both mounted;
Ras Makonnen, Fitawrari Gebeihu, Qanyazmatch Tafessa,
Dejazmatch Chacha; Abuna Matewos and church procession

the Battle of Adowa
purchased in 1906 by Alfred Ilg, Menelik's Swiss advisor

Aleqa Eleyas

Staatliche Museen für Völkerkunde
Berlin, Germany

Battle of Adwa

Mingei International Museum of World Folk Art
San Diego, California, USA

Mingei International Museum of World Folk Art
San Diego, California, USA

the Emperor and warriors

the Battle of Adowa

Aleqa Eleyas

acquired in 1910 by Swiss traveler, George Montandant
Ville de Neuchâtel Musée D'Ethnographie
Neuchâtel, Switzerland

Menelik at the Battle of Adwa, 1896 A.D.

Afework Tekle

Taitu 1890 A.D.

Afework Tekle

statue of Menelik II in Addis Ababa, Ethiopia photograph by Tesfai Biftu

photograph by Tesfai Biftu

statue of Menelik II in Addis Ababa, Ethiopia today

defender of his country, Adwa

Afework Tekle 1977

Afework Tekle 1987

defender of his country, Afar

Menelik's statue

Fasil Dawit 1995

Fasil Dawit 1995

mountains of Adwa

Emperor Menelik

Fasil Dawit 1995

How the News was Received in England

Richard Pankhurst

The English "man in the street," who until then had been profoundly unaware of Italian diplomatic maneuvers to annex Ethiopia, opened his newspaper some one hundred years ago to a shocking report. He learned that, for the first time since the Carthagian Hannibal marched into the valley of the Po two thousand years earlier, an army from Africa had decisively defeated a large and well equipped European force. How these events were presented to the British public by *The Times*, and how that semiofficial newspaper explained what it considered to be the interest of the British Government is revealing.

The dramatic news from Africa resulted in the immediate collapse of the Italian government of Signor Crispi, considered responsible for the defeat. Newspapers throughout the world were confronted almost simultaneously with exciting war reports and with news of an Italian cabinet crisis. The Rome government had of course been deeply implicated in the Ethiopian war. Only a few days before the battle, *The Times* had published a report from its Rome correspondent highlighting Franco-Italian jealousy over the intended partition of the Horn of Africa. It asserted that the Italian government was aware of "a secret treaty" between France and Ethiopia in which the French were supporting Menelik in order to embarrass Italy. The Paris *Temps* immediately denied what it called this "extraordinary" report. A dispatch from the Paris correspondent of *The Times* made it apparent that colonially minded sections of French public opinion, though opposed to Italy as a rival colonial power, were unwilling to side with the invaded country because it was on the African continent.

> *No one here—I have not to take notice of this or that scatter-brained person, or a few habitually malevolent minds—wishes for the success of the Abyssinians at the price of the discomfiture of a civilized nation, from which it is quite possible to differ in aims and opinions without being supposed to cherish any ill-will when that nation is face to face with a brave but barbarous foe.*

Despite these words, the Paris correspondent confirmed a tendency in French circles to be "rather kindly disposed" toward "the presence of serious difficulties for Italy in Africa." He was confident however that the "somewhat bitter complaints" of the Italian politicians would "induce no revival of hostility" against Italy in France.

The great Ethiopian victory changed the entire picture. *The Times*, which until then had referred to the Ethiopians as a "barbarous foe," now scolded General Baratieri for imagining he confronted "undisciplined and ill-armed savages." A few days later the newspaper declared that the Ethiopians were "a civilized power both in the way they made war and in the way they conducted their diplomacy." On March 6 it discussed the Italian political crisis in the following words:

> *Though the Crispi Government cannot be held directly responsible for the Italian defeat at Adwa, it was certain that General Baratieri's blunder would bring about its overthrow ... Signor Crispi's action appears to have the approval of moderate men ... but the extreme Left, enraged by the curtailment of its opportunities for vituperation, has not been able to control its temper either within the Chamber or outside. The sitting seems to have closed in hopeless confusion, while Radical Deputies placed themselves at the head of excited mobs, marching through the streets with loud cries for the impeachment of the fallen Ministers. It is, happily, difficult for human nature to remain long at fever heat. The very violence of these demonstrations tends to shorten their duration, so that after a certain amount of shouting, gesticulating and anathematizing, we may expect the Piazza Colonna to regain its wonted calm and the people to regain the rational consideration of events.*

Reporting that the Marquis di Rudini had set up what was to prove a merely interim administration, the newspaper alluded to other Italian problems:

> *While the excitement in Rome arises naturally out of the profound chagrin with which a sensitive people receives the news of a great calamity, there are threats of disturbance in other parts of Italy which are of a more disquieting character. In Sicily there is chronic disaffection, which, it will be remembered, was not long ago suppressed or driven under by Signor Crispi. His fall in circumstances so deplorable will undoubtedly prove a great encouragement to all the disorderly factions ... It*

from *The Graphic*, April 11, 1896 New York, New York

view from the south of the fortified Italian camp at Adwa, captured by the Abyssinians must therefore be hoped by all friends of Italy that, whether under the Marquis di Rudini or another, a Government may be promptly formed capable of steadily maintaining the authority of the laws.

Despite the hopes of such "friends of Italy," riots were reported from Rome, Naples, Milan and the other principal cities. A telegram even reached London, reporting the assassination of ex-prime minister Crispi. On the following day, March 7, it was learned however that this report was unfounded, a *Times* editorial declaring:

... the good name of the Italian people has not been dishonoured in its hour of trial by the crime of a maddened mob. [The editorial went on to recall that] the Italians today [were] the descendants and the heirs of the people whose Senate thanked an erring and defeated General, after the crushing disaster of Cannae because he had not despaired of the Republic. [The newspaper would] not permit [itself] to discuss the possibility that the (Savoyan) dynasty may be threatened [as] a revolution in Italy would be unspeakably calamitous to the country itself and would menace the tranquillity of the whole of Europe.

These arguments were used again almost half a century later when it was thought that action by the League of Nations might bring Mussolini's invasion of Ethiopia in 1935–36 to a halt. Advising the Italian people not to display such "ingratitude" to King Humbert, whose father had "played so noble a part in winning and consolidating Italian unity and freedom," *The Times* advised a policy of caution and compromise as best calculated to serve Italian interests in Africa:

What is to be deprecated in the interests of Italy is the hasty and inconsiderate adoption of a policy of extremes. Some of her counselors support the present outcry of the populace for an immediate and unconditional retirement from Abyssinia. Others exhort her at all costs to wipe out what is represented as a stain upon her honour by renewing her military and financial efforts on a greater scale than ever. Both courses, in our opinion, are equally unwise. A complete and precipitate withdrawal would be surely and

reinforcements leaving the railway station at Massawa (after the defeat at Adwa) speedily repented, and the responsibility for it would be urged against the King's Government at no distant date by those whose interest it is to create troubles. On the other hand, it is absurd to say that the honour of Italy can only be secured by undertaking the conquest of Abyssinia—a task which would not be hopefully attempted in the existing state of public opinion. Her true policy would appear to be that of withdrawing from the mountain region where General Baratieri met his ruin, as well as from Kassala, where she is threatened by the Dervishes, and holding Massawah with the dominating positions in the neighborhood, as a pied-à-terre from which to watch events. Thus the present might be made safe while the future would not be compromised.

However "natural" the impulse "to pour in men and munitions" to avenge the defeat, the political horizon was "not so clear." *The Times* added a few days later that Italy could not

afford to entangle herself in adventures which there is no hope of carrying to a successful issue except by means of exhausting expenditure and persevering effort.

Meanwhile the Parliamentary crisis dragged on in Italy while more detailed news of the failure at Adwa flooded in. On March 9 *The Times* had a lot to say on both subjects. Discussing the battle, particulars of which had at last reached England, the newspaper seemed almost to be fighting the engagement a second time. It went to considerable length to point out Baratieri's tactical errors. Being pro-Italian, it repeatedly referred to the Ethiopian army as "the Shoans," though in fact all the principal provinces of Ethiopia were included in the armies at Adwa, and in particular the Tigray, whom the Italians had tried hard to detach from its loyalty to the Ethiopian empire.

The Times' account is as follows:

The latest accounts place the Italian loss in the battle of Adwa at a figure so high that we cannot but hope there is a serious mistake somewhere. It is estimated at no less than 7,000 white and 2,000 native troops, though what proportion of the missing are killed and how many are prisoners it is at present impossible to

from *The Graphic*, April 11, 1896 New York, New York

the port of Adigrat, where an Italian garrison was besieged by the Abyssinians

say. As the total number of troops engaged in the attack is given as 15,000 and cannot have been very easily in excess of that number, the disaster has clearly been one of quite exceptional magnitude. One-half the forces, and, if the figures are correct, much more than one-half seem to have disappeared. Italians will find a melancholy consolation in the fact that their troops fought with desperate gallantry. One division seems to have been practically destroyed where it stood, after inflicting enormous loss upon the enemy. It was probably owing to the severity of their punishment that the Shoans abstained in a manner otherwise unaccountable from a pursuit which might have rendered the catastrophe even more appalling. They have evidently not followed up their victory for Adigrat is invested, and the position of its garrison renders the whole situation infinitely more difficult to deal with. Adigrat is not upon the direct line of retreat, and General Baratieri seems to have been too hard pressed either to turn aside and avoid leaving the road to Asmara open to the Abyssinians, or even to give the garrison timely notice of its impending isolation. With 600 sick in hospital its movements were seriously hampered, and the enemy seem to have been within a

Menelik and the troops at dawn awaiting the Italian attack

Fasil Dawit 1995

few kilometers before the commander was aware of his danger. From the tone of his message it may be doubted whether he is even now acquainted with the full extent of his disaster, for he speaks cheerfully of having a month's provisions. So far as can be judged at the present there is little chance of relief reaching Adigrat within a month in face of what is plainly a forward movement on the part of the Abyssinians.

While the Italian troops displayed splendid valour, their generals seem to have set at defiance all the elementary rules of warfare, and especially of mountain warfare. The Shoan army was posted upon an elevated plateau to the number, it is said, of 80,000 men. General Baratieri must have had abundant opportunities of learning of their equipment and the use they could make of it, consequently he can hardly have imagined that he was dealing with undisciplined and ill-armed savages. Yet he behaved as if nothing were in front of him but a rabble which would melt away on contact with disciplined troops. He attacked that plateau with three divisions, marching through three valleys or ravines and therefore completely isolated and incapable of mutual support. He neglected the elementary rule never to engage your forces in a defile without occupying the hills that command it. The rocky heights that effectively separated his columns were taken possession of by the Shoans with the utmost facility, because they practically entered on the level. They could therefore flank each of General Baratieri's divisions, which struggling in the narrow passes, had no room for the evolutions required to offer even such defense as was possible against such odds. To attack such an enemy at all on the front was a serious blunder, but to attack in that particular manner shows an almost incredible disregard of the rudimentary principles of military science. The motives which impelled General Baratieri to push forward regardless of the danger to which he exposed his reinforcements he knew to be on the way, and to make his ill-judged attack without awaiting their arrival, almost baffle conjecture. It would, however, be well to await further details before attributing his impatience purely to personal motives. Italy is not the only Power which on political or religious pretexts interests herself in Abyssinia, and it is just conceivable that there were political motives for pressing the unfortunate General to score some success if possible, even at the serious risk of failure.

Turning to the political situation in Italy, the newspaper announced that Signor Saracco had failed in his efforts to form a cabinet. It continued:

On the immediate question of the policy to be pursued in Abyssinia, the Cabinet will have to come to a decision which, whatever its nature, will arouse opposition from one side or another. Each of the three possible policies has it advocates. With a large section of the nation the whole Abyssinian enterprise is unpopular, and nothing short of complete abandonment would satisfy some critics. On the other hand, the feelings of a high-spirited people are profoundly stirred by the crushing reverse at Adwa, which to many will seem to call for the most determined efforts to regain the position that has been lost. Between these two is the middle course which we have ventured to urge upon the Italian Government, that of rigorous concentration within an area capable of being defended without excessive effort.

Elaborating this proposal, the editorial concluded:

Italy need not abandon any of her claims or renounce any project that careful consideration may show to be feasible. But in the meantime a defensive and waiting policy seems to be clearly indicated alike by military and political motives.

The Times deeply regretted a European army being decisively defeated by a "native" force. It stressed the difference between the Ethiopians and other inhabitants of Africa, then also confronted with imperialist pressure. The Ethiopians, a civilized power should, therefore, not be confused with "savage tribes incapable of making a stand against a regular European attack."

Discussing the outcome of the campaign *The Times* added:

It was true that, in some respects, the military disaster seems to be less crushing than was supposed. The Abyssinian generals do not appear to have followed up their victory with the vigor enjoined by all the masters of the art of war. Hence the actual destruction of the Italian forces is less complete than it might easily have been and has been assumed to be.

Moreover, considerable numbers of stragglers were turning up at Italian headquarters. The newspaper continued:

Unfortunately this is about the only gleam of consolation that can be found in the story of a most disastrous enterprise. Though the men remain, the army has sustained a deadly blow. Such a reverse, accompanied by heavy loss of artillery, cannot but prove demoralizing to any force and specially to one largely composed of native levies. The more we learn about the matter, the more serious does it become from this point of view.

These comments merely served to strengthen the newspaper's conviction that it would be "unwise" for Italy to attempt a policy of immediate revenge. It added:

Were the Shoan army to make an energetic forward movement, it would be difficult to assign limits to the embarrassments of the Italian Government.

Emperor Menelik confined his advance to the frontier existing at the time Fitawrari Makonnen signed in Rome on Ethiopia's behalf the annex to the Treaty of Uccialli [Wuchale]—even though the Italians by trickery had advanced that frontier beyond the line they occupied when the treaty was signed.

The attitude of *The Times* was thus one of friendship for the aggressor, qualified only by a criticism of Italian tactical mistakes. Thus it declared that the Italians had

to do more than merely reconsider the plan of operations followed, under considerable pressure from home, by General Baratieri. They have to revise their whole policy towards Abyssinia, and if on mature consideration they think it necessary to attempt the conquest of the country, they must make up their minds to efforts very much greater and more exhausting than they have hitherto contemplated.

Developing this same train of thought the editorial concluded:

It is felt at this moment, in every European capital, that the position in Italy is critical, and her action is watched, if with varying sympathies, at all events with unvarying closeness of attention. A mere African expedition against nomad tribes would not affect her general position or call forth all this anxiety. It is seen that she is involved in an enterprise of a totally different kind which, if persevered in, cannot but profoundly affect all her European relations. Her allies of the Triple Alliance are exhibiting the most unmistakable symptoms of concern.

Discussing the British attitude the newspaper was brutally frank:

The sympathies of this country cannot be thought doubtful for an instant. Englishmen have a sincere and enduring friendship for Italy, while English policy regards her as an essential and most valuable factor in the political equilibrium of Europe. Her aims in Abyssinia we in this country regard without the faintest tinge of jealousy, while her general well-being, political and financial, is earnestly desired.

The Times' stated that Ethiopia was a "civilized power," both in her methods of warfare and in her diplomacy. But this contradicted the paper's sympathetic stance toward Italy and the legitimacy of Italy's unprovoked and unscrupulous aggression and the further assertion that she "need not abandon her claims," but rather should bide her time to strike again at Ethiopian freedom at some favorable opportunity. Italy's claim to govern Ethiopia was based on a trick—the inclusion in the Italian version of the Treaty of Wuchale of words that were not in the Ethiopian version. British sympathy for Italian aggression had three motives:

1. hope that Italian expansion would prevent the French from gaining influence in the area;
2. desire to win Italian support in the Mediterranean; and
3. fear that the defeat of a European power by an African nation would create unrest in British colonies.

When order was at last established in Italy, *The Times* devoted a March 11 leading article to expressing its thankfulness that the Italian government had adopted the course of action the paper had been recommending. *The Times* declared:

> *After the first outburst of national grief and disappointment men are settling down to calm and earnest consideration of the condition of affairs ... Popular demonstrations against the despatch of reinforcements to Massawa have given place to a general conviction that, whatever decision may be ultimately arrived at as to Italian policy, it is indispensable that General Baldissera [Baratieri's successor] should receive all the support he may deem necessary. Those responsible, whether immediately or approximately, for the disaster of Adwa, will undoubtedly be called to account in good time. But for the moment the more pressing duty is to effect the relief of the garrisons ignored.*

On a projected Italian campaign against Harar it commented:

> *The point of most interest to ourselves in the documents is the account they give of the negotiations opened up by Italy in respect of Zeila. The Italians, at one period of the campaign, believed that by landing troops at that port and marching them in the direction of Harar, they could distract the attention of the Abyssinians and divert a portion of their forces from the theater of operations further north. General Ferrero, the Italian Ambassador in this country, was instructed to ask our permission for the landing of the troops. The British Government were quite willing and even anxious to give the Italians any aid they rightly could give them, but the objection to the proposal was obvious. It was possible that the column operating from Zeila might be repulsed and driven back upon Somaliland.*

Were we to endanger a British possession from a desire to assist a friendly people?

Moreover, there was another diplomatic obstacle—the opposition of France. *The Times* continues:

> *France regarded the project with intense jealousy, and we were naturally reluctant to give her any just grounds of offense, either of a general kind or arising from our agreement with her in regard to Harar itself. These topics were discussed with the freedom usual in diplomatic conversations of a confidential nature between Lord Salisbury and General Ferrero, in London, and between Sir Clare Ford and Baron Blanc, in Rome ... The project was received, and in January of the present year Lord Salisbury assented to the passage of the Italian troops through Zeila while making reservations to spare any just susceptibilities on the part of France. At various points in the negotiation of this extremely difficult and complex affair, our Government were not able at once to accept the view of the Italians, and on one occasion especially Baron Blanc, in conversation with the British Ambassador in Rome, signified his annoyance in very plain terms. Exaggerated language was employed, and in possible contingencies action was spoken of which, doubtless, it was never intended to carry out. These conversations have been published in the Green Book, and it is difficult to suppose that they can have been published with any object but one. That object certainly was not to inform the Italian people as to what the relations between Great Britain and Italy really were at the close of the Crispi Administration. Those relations were always friendly, as they are friendly now. They depend on interests too deep and solid to be affected by petty questions in remote parts of Africa. Our friendship rests upon our common interests and our common objectives in the Mediterranean, and while those remain it can never be shaken.*

Prime Minister Crispi

Marquis di Rudini

The Italian Crisis

A PERFECT sea of troubles has overwhelmed Italy since the crushing blow fell in Abyssinia. The humiliation of her military defeat is made still more bitter by the fierce revolutionary agitation shaking the throne and the dread of losing her position among the nations. Rarely indeed has a country been in so grave a strait. Poverty and public feeling alike demand the reversal of the aggressive African policy, yet to retreat without retrieving her prestige seems intolerable to Italy. Thus, though the Crispi Cabinet has collapsed, the present Rudini-Ricotti Ministry are positively arranging to carry out much of their predecessors' schemes which they denounced so hotly in Opposition. Reinforcements and artillery are being despatched in response to General Baldissera's urgent demands till the hopes of the new Ministry being a Cabinet of Peace wax faint. There is no doubt about popular opinion in the matter. Scarcely one Italian town of importance has been free from the most outspoken demonstrations against continuing the campaign, while in some cases crowds have tried to stop the soldiers starting for Africa. Moreover, the troops themselves strongly object to leave. Loyalty to the Savoy dynasty is sadly weakened by recent events, while Signor Crispi is just now the best hated man in Italy. It is neatly said that Adowa has proved his Sadowa.

Meanwhile the Italian situation in Abyssinia is most precarious. Fortunately for the Italians, Menelik's victorious army are in no more hurry to follow up their advantage than before, so that it has been possible for the bulk of the invaders to draw together nearer safety. The most anxious points are Kassala and Adigrat. Orders have been sent to the Kassala garrison to withdraw, but this is easier said than done, with the dervishes hovering round, emboldened by the Abyssinian success. Adigrat is invested by two formidable Shoan columns, and as the place is well fortified and armed, the Commander declares that he can hold out for a month by economising provisions. So General Baldissera is trying to concentrate forces within the triangle formed by Keren, Asmara, and Massowah, hoping to march to the relief of Adigrat and Kassala directly he receives sufficient help from home. Menelik himself is said to be eager to make peace, being strongly opposed to fighting a Christian army. But King Humbert is far from ready to meet him half way if there be any truth in the statement that the King has declared he will never negotiate with the Negus. General Baratieri, the ex-Commander-in-Chief, is to go home under arrest, and from the details of the battle of Adowa now to hand it is considered that the general's bad strategy and arrangement of the forces led to the disaster. He divided his army into three isolated columns instead of concentrating his strength, placed them in narrow ravines, where they had no room to manœuvre, and neglected the elementary precaution of occupying the hills above. The scouting system seems to have been equally faulty, so that the main body did not know the need of going to their comrades' help. As to the Italian troops, their bravery deserves the highest praise. They fought to the last gasp, particularly the Alpine regiments. Generals Albertone and Dabormida were fairly cut to pieces in the midst of their men, and among the most gallant officers who fell was young Prince Chigi, scion of a famous Roman house. Stragglers are still coming in to the Italian camp, but the total loss is estimated at 7,000 at least. The Shoans have many prisoners, including General Arimondi.

Foreign sympathy has not failed Italy in her day of need. Even France has almost ignored the long estrangement to express most cordial sentiments towards her much-tried neighbour, though a few discordant notes are struck.

Some Diplomatic Consequences: Europe, Ethiopia and The Sudan

Richard Pankhurst

The Italian defeat on March 1, 1896 at the Battle of Adwa was so crushing that the Crispi government collapsed. The session of the Chamber of Deputies in Rome ended in confusion. Radical deputies led excited mobs through the town demanding the impeachment of the fallen ministers. Riots also broke out in Naples, Milan and other towns. In Eritrea the defeated Baratieri was replaced by General Baldissera.

The German government complained that England had not come to Italy's aid in her predicament. Lord Salisbury replied that if his government proposed financial aid to Italy, the English bankers would protest. And besides, any other steps taken to aid Italy would probably provoke an Ethiopian attack on Zeila. In Cairo the German ambassador discussed "Job's news from Abyssinia" with Lord Cromer, who represented British power in Egypt. "When he expressed regret at the Italian defeat," wrote the German ambassador, "I told him without circumlocution that England ought to have given help a long time ago." After a week of crisis Crispi's successor, Rudini, formed a government pledged to make peace in Africa.

A treaty of "perpetual peace and friendship between Italy and Ethiopia" was therefore signed on October 26, 1896. It declared the Treaty of Wuchale "definitely annulled." Italy recognized the independence, "absolute and without reserve," of the empire of Ethiopia as "a sovereign independent state." To prevent any ambiguity it was specified in the treaty that its contents must be made known to all powers who had been notified by Italy of the alleged protectorate. The text of the treaty was written in French and Amharic. Menelik refused to accept any Italian text. (He had trusted advisors who spoke French.) The Italians agreed they would never cede any of their colonies bordering Ethiopia to any other power and that, in case they ever wished to abandon any such possession, it would revert to Ethiopia.

Italy however kept the colony of Eritrea, including Keren and Asmara, and extending to the Mareb. The Italians had brought in numerous reinforcements to maintain their "first born" colony. Had Menelik sought to advance further, his enemies would almost certainly have received support from other colonial powers.

Perhaps providentially in view of the colonial world's general hostility, Menelik and his counselors decided that continuing the fight beyond Adwa was too perilous for Ethiopia. The continued Italian occupation of the coast had to be accepted, and Italy preserved a base for a further war of aggression thirty-eight years later.

Even as it was, the result of the battle caused great excitement in Europe. In Paris the *Temps* declared that the news was nothing less than "extraordinary." *La Liberté* observed that the Italians "without intending it had brought Ethiopia out of its shell." The newspaper continued:

> *All European countries will be obliged to make a place for this new brother who steps forth ready to play in the Dark Continent the role of Japan in the Far East ... The Negus is destined to be an unexpected factor in the war which the Europeans are waging in the land of Shem, a factor destined to modify the theory of the Hinterland and others as false as that famous Bull of Pope Alexander VI dividing the unknown world between Spain and Portugal against which Francis I, as a descendant of Adam, protested.*

G.F.H. Berkeley, who in 1902 wrote a well documented account of the battle, wondered whether it did not "herald the rise of a new power in Africa." He added,

> *We are reminded that the natives of that continent may yet become a military factor worthy of our closest attention. The suggestion has been made—absurd as it appears at present—that this is the first revolt of the Dark Continent against domineering Europe.*

Throughout the campaign the European powers were deeply alarmed at the possibility of an Ethiopian-Sudanese reconciliation. This likelihood was first suggested to the Italian government by their ambassador to Russia. The British prime minister, Lord Salisbury, was not sure whether the rumor of joint action against Italy by the Ethiopians and Sudanese was true or not. But he was quick to express the view that an attack by the Khalifah against the Italians at Kassala was not improbable. As early as January 11, 1896 he had corresponded with Lord Cromer on the possibility of armed intervention to prevent such development.

Do you think that demonstration in the neighbourhood of Wadi Halfa would be useful to create a diversion and do you see any objection to such a step being taken?

Cromer at first replied that no demonstration would appreciably affect the Italian position and that a conquest of the Sudan would be more useful than a mere demonstration. If territory were occupied and then abandoned, it would enhance the prestige of the Dervishes. A month later, however, he wrote that after consulting the military authorities he had worked out a plan designed to stop the Dervish advance on Italian territories. "It is on every ground most undesirable," he wrote, "that the Dervishes should be allowed to re-establish themselves as Kassala. If anything is to be done, prompt action is necessary."

The Ethiopian victory at Adwa entirely transformed the situation. It became obvious on the one hand that the Dervishes had a chance of investing Kassala. On the other hand, the French were liable to increase their influence in the "power vacuum" created by the Italian defeat. On March 2, the day after the battle, news reached Cairo that the Dervishes had fired on the fort. On March 10 the British ambassador in Rome telegraphed to the prime minister that the fort was completely surrounded and all communication cut. Two days later Salisbury received a request from the Italian ambassador in London to authorize a diversion by Egyptian troops. (Egypt was then under British occupation.) Salisbury told the ambassador that Cromer had at last been given instructions authorizing an advance to Dongola. The telegram to Cromer ran as follows:

The Italian Ambassador has pressed me earnestly to take some steps against the Dervishes in favor of Kassala. After consulting the military authorities Her Majesty's government are of the opinion that the occupation of Dongola would be the most effective demonstration, and that the measure will be greatly in the interest of Egypt, and is a charge she may fairly be asked to bear. It will also tend to repel any disposition to attack Egypt which the recent victories over Europeans may have created among the Dervishes. Of course, it is intended to keep Dongola. The War Office is communicating with the military authorities. No secrecy is at all necessary.

from *Harper's Weekly* 1896 New York, New York

troops assembling for muster

The European powers were deeply alarmed by the signs of cooperation between Menelik and the Khalifah. The Rome *Tribuna* declared it

> *... certain that an agreement exists between our two enemies. After the Sahati campaign Yohannes wrote to the Khalifah inviting him to come to an agreement with him to drive the Europeans into the sea. Then the Khalifah was too strong to accept the advice, and was still too much a slave to religious fanaticism to be able to come to terms with the infidel ... Now religious fanaticism is conquered ... So we have had almost in the same day the news that Menelik had informed the Khalifah of his victory at Adwa and that among the Dervishes killed in the unsuccessful attack on Zabderat were mingled Abyssinians. "I have beaten the Italians in Adwa" wrote the Negus. "It is now your turn to conquer them at Kassala."*

The Times commented on March 13:

> *It need hardly be said that any Egyptian demonstration beyond the frontier must be of assistance to the Italians in the gallant struggle they are carrying on in Abyssinia; and that Her Majesty's government must have had this desirable object in view in assenting to a forward move by the Egyptian troops. The Italians are, unfortunately, engaged simultaneously with two enemies who might conceivably with different management have been played off against one another ... the present position of the Kassala garrison must be a serious addition to the cares of General Baldissera, and anything that improves its prospects naturally leaves him so much more free to deal with the Shoans who are now pressing the Italian forces rather hard.*

Six days later, an editorial in the same paper, announcing the capture of Kassala, declared:

> *If the serious news that Kassala has been abandoned is correct, Italy will need all the more urgently any*

diversion which it is possible to afford her in other quarters.

Thus began the operations that resulted in the reconquest first of Dongola and then of the entire Sudan (1896–1900).

"If Italy had won at Adwa," writes professor Ernest Work, "there would certainly have been no such hasty movements of British and Egyptian troops at Dongola." But, he continues

> *... since Italy, England's accomplice in the plot, was not to have control in Ethiopia, it was clear to the government of Her Britannic Majesty that the whole eastern part, if not the whole Nile valley, was exposed to the avarice of other European Powers, none of whom, at that time, could be looked upon as England's friend. This, of course, would endanger the Cape-to-Cairo dreams and threaten the water supply to the Nile valley. Salisbury's government evidently thought that the time had come to comply with the demands of the London Chamber of Commerce to "take adequate measures with a view to assuring the control of England over the whole valley of the Nile from Uganda to Fashoda."*

British action was deeply influenced by rivalry with France. As soon as the news of the Battle of Adwa reached Paris, the French felt confident they could maintain their influence in Ethiopia. They therefore made preparations to extend their control of West Africa to the upper Nile with the object of moving French forces to the western borders of Ethiopia. A mission left France in three sections on April 25, May 10 and May 15, though its leader Captain Marchand did not leave Marseilles until June 25 when he set sail with orders to continue to Fashoda on the Nile. Meanwhile, in Ethiopia, French engineers began work on a railway from Djibouti to Addis Ababa in accordance with a concession that had been obtained in 1894. To join hands with Marchand's expedition, a group of French officers organized a party of about two hundred Ethiopians at Mount Menagasha, some miles west of Addis Ababa with instructions to establish a fort on the right bank of the Nile.

Developments in Ethiopia and the Sudan were closely intertwined throughout this period. As soon as Dongola was effectively brought under control, the British learned that a Franco-Ethiopian force was advancing toward the upper waters of the Nile. They also learned that an Ethiopian mission had been well received by the Khalifah. A British mission under Sir Rennell Rodd was accordingly dispatched to Addis Ababa in 1897. It had the dual task of reducing French influence at the Ethiopian court and destroying any possible agreement that might have been made between Menelik and the Khalifah. The mission reported that the Khalifah had sent ambassadors to Menelik who were lodged in the house of Archbishop Mathios, but not permitted to hold communication with unauthorized persons. Though Rodd was unwilling to recognize Menelik's proposed frontiers of Ethiopia, conversations proceeded in a friendly manner.

The French minister, M. Lagarde, had an advantage over his British rival. His country had aided Menelik against Italy while Britain had been pro-Italian and had schemed for the attempted partition of the country. Lagarde moreover gave his full approval of Menelik's frontiers and even urged the emperor to extend them westward to link up with Marchand's area of expansion. The Frenchman therefore succeeded in persuading Menelik to sign a Franco-Ethiopian alliance on March 20, 1897. However, a treaty with England was also signed on May 14 in which Menelik agreed to maintain a friendly attitude toward the forthcoming British operations in the Sudan. Article VI of the Anglo-Ethiopian Agreement of 1897 stated that

> *the Emperor engages himself towards the government of Her Majesty to do all in his power to prevent the passage through his dominions of arms and ammunition to the Mahdists, whom he declares to be the enemies of his Empire.*

The frontiers between Ethiopia and the British Somaliland protectorate were defined and Ethiopia was permitted freely to import state material through the port of Zeila, northwest of Hargeisa.

Meanwhile, the French expedition from Addis Ababa to the Nile ran into so many difficulties that it had to be abandoned, although by the end of 1897 four Ethiopian columns were moving westward under the commands of Ras Makonnen, Ras Tessema, Ras Wolde Giorgis and Ras Habte Giorgis. Despite considerable obstacles Ras Tessema reached the Nile, south of Sobat, raising the Ethiopian flag on the right bank on June 20, 1898. At the same time, a Frenchman, M. Faivre, swam to an island midstream where he hoisted the French tricolor as a sign of French sovereignty. Fever among his troops however forced Ras Tessema to move to higher altitudes, obliging him to leave the Nile less than two weeks before Marchand floated down the river—passing the very spot on which the French flag had been flown. On reaching Fashoda the Frenchman therefore found no friendly outstretched hand reaching across the Nile as he expected. Instead a British force under Kitchener arrived by gunboat on September 19.

Sir Reginald Wingate, who accompanied this force, describes how the British insisted on raising the Egyptian flag at Fashoda. Though the French opposed Britain they found it difficult to object to a reassertion of Egyptian claims in the area. Wingate and Kitchener accordingly wore Egyptian uniform, the latter also donning a fez. Wrote Wingate:

> *As we were slowly steaming towards Fashoda we espied a small row boat coming down with an immense French flag in the bows. She came alongside and a black sergeant came on board and presented Marchand's reply which was to the effect that he had reached Fashoda on 10th July, that he had the orders of the French government to occupy the Bahr el Ghazal and Fashoda, which he had done ... he said he had made a Treaty with the Mek of the Shilluks by which the latter had placed the whole of his country under French protection, and that he had sent copies of this Treaty to his government by way of Abyssinia and via the Bahr el Ghazal ...*
>
> *... on arrival at Fashoda, Marchand and Captain Germain came onboard and we four solemnly sat down to discuss the situation ... Kitchener spoke well, telling Marchand that this might mean war between France and England; he asked Marchand whether in face of our vastly preponderating strength he intended to resist Egypt reasserting its rights over its former possession and the hoisting of the Egyptian flag, and Marchand replied that of course he could not do so, but that he could not himself retire without the orders of his government ...*

I then went all round the French position with Germain and eventually selected a spot on which to hoist the Egyptian flag ... We then turned out all the troops, had a solemn ceremony of hoisting the flag, fired a salute of 21 guns, appointed Jackson Commandant of Fashoda and left a big garrison with him. Thus our poor French friends are virtually our prisoners ... of course we gave them formal protests against their occupation of Fashoda and the presence of the French in any part of the Nile valley, and we made regulations prohibiting the transport of all war material in the Nile ... Marchand told me French, Russians and Abyssinians had come down the Sorbat, where they had made treaties with the tribes, given them Abyssinian flags and established an Abyssinian protectorate.

News of the Fashoda incident created great excitement in Europe. It seemed for a moment that hostilities might break out between the two powers, though the French were at a considerable disadvantage as their fleet was far inferior to the British navy. The Dreyfus affair had moreover hopelessly divided French public opinion, with the result that the country was in no mood for war. In November the French government ordered Marchand's withdrawal. He passed through Ethiopia and Djibouti where he received a triumphal welcome.

The French surrender at Fashoda marked the end of major Anglo-French rivalry in Africa. Talks between the two countries began on January 21, 1899 to prevent future events from occurring while defining the two countries' respective spheres of influence. The path was now clear for the Entente Cordiale of 1904 whereby Britain backed France in Morocco and France supported Britain in Egypt. The old nineteenth century rivalry between Britain and France was giving way to the new twentieth century rivalry in which Britain, France and Russia would one day unite against Germany, Austria and Turkey.

Crazy Tale, a historical fiction

Amare Tegbaru

My father like his father, my father's father like his father's father—the telling of the story of our country and our people is endless. Once he starts he never stops. He keeps on going and going. As for me, I preferred listening to this story from my grandfather, not my father. When my father was born my grandfather was old, though an astute and intelligent man. Unfortunately he died when I was quite young. But I remember it all.

While I listen he pauses often to see if I am paying attention. He says "OK! and!" I want to respond, but every time I repeat after him, "OK! and!," it sounds as though I am making fun of him. But if I don't respond, how will he know I am attentively listening?

Mother stares at me. A few moments ago she looked so busy with her daily work, moving around the room, making *injera* bread while listening to the stories. I never noticed my mother observing me. Suddenly she's upset.

"My son. When you listen to him say 'um! aha!' don't let him recount these events as though he was talking to himself. In fact it would be wise to write it all down now so that you won't forget it."

Grandfather always told stories in a long, roundabout way. Often he remembered events by saint's day or the war campaign in the various regions. It was hard to follow his stories.

Now he is old. Seeing him lying in bed, he just looks helpless. It was during the Italian invasion in World War II that he was wounded by a fascist bullet that left him partially paralyzed. Many say he fought bravely in the thick of that battle. My mother feels sorry to see him lying in his lonely bed.

The task of looking after my grandfather is immense. My mother moves him from one side to the other. Because he can't move himself, the burden is on her. Though difficult, she takes it upon herself to pay for the sacrifices my grandfather made to preserve our freedom and independence. She is closer to him than his own son. They like each other. She often says, "Your grandfather was an outstanding hero at the Battle of Adwa."

When grandfather died and his body was taken out for burial, my mother, weeping, went berserk. However my father, his son, suppressed his feelings, kept his temper, didn't show the blow he had received. He acted as though his manhood would be questioned if he wept like my mother. He didn't beat his chest nor did he threaten to be buried with his father—like my mother. He didn't wish, like her, for the earth to open up and swallow him. My grandfather's death seemed like the death of my mother's father, not my father's father.

◆-◆-◆

"Enat!" my grandfather called my mother.

"Enat Alem?" my father responded. "Enat Alem went to the market today—Thursday, market day. Did you forget?"

"No! It's just force of habit, since I call her for everything."

Father asked if he wanted to be moved. Grandfather said yes.

After my father moved him, grandfather said, "Because Enat was young I thought she was stronger, able to move me every hour." Breathing heavily my father moved grandfather again. Then he asked if there was a special reason why Enat went to the market today—besides that it's Thursday.

"Yes," my father replied. "Saint George's Day is coming on the twenty-third and she wanted to buy barley and hops to make *tella* (beer) and *tej* (honey wine)."

Since my grandfather always observed Saint George's Day, he looked downcast, deep in thought. I suppose he was thinking about when he was very young and followed Dejazmatch Basha Aboye from the Amhara land to join Menelik's expedition force to expel the Italian invaders. My grandfather struggled to hold his tears whenever he talked about the Battle of Adwa. Ethiopia's victory at Amba Alage and Makelle upset the Italians so much that they came back for revenge later.

They never talked about the 1940s war they both fought in against the Italian invaders. When my grandfather started to talk about the Battle of Adwa, he would take practically the whole day. His memories would fill him with passion, and he grieved, remembering his fallen friends, gallant fighters all. Often he used dramatic facial gestures to show the pain of battle.

Father would detect when I became restless. He would say to me, "Fekadu don't start again. You children of today have no patience." The truth is, I am not really a child of today. But to him, I was always a child. "To hear the history of our ancient land would be a blessing. But you worship everything from Europe. If I were in your place," he said, "I should consider it a gift to be able to hear it. In a country where the benefits of independence are not revealed to the population, it would be wise for you to listen to what our ancestors have been telling us. This opportunity may not come again. You have been going to school. So, tell me the history of our country. What have you learned?" my father asked.

I was honestly dumbfounded. I didn't know what to answer. But from that moment, I began to really hear the stories my grandfather told. Carrying my pencil and notebook I diligently listened and wrote down everything he said.

It was after that conversation that I understood the significance of the victory at Adwa and how it created such a pride in our people. Even now—crazy as I am—I have the notes I took so many years ago. Everything he observed at the Battle of Adwa was documented. It is these stories that I, Fekadu Molla, kept. I have tried to tell anyone I could, especially after I lost my mind.

◆-◆-◆

When the European educational system was introduced in Ethiopia, all the schools taught in French. Fekadu Molla was one of those few students who completed fifth grade at the Menelik boarding school. He showed a great love for drama, poetry and acting. At a parents' days celebration, the school put on a play about the Battle of Adwa in front of His Imperial Majesty Haile Selassie I. Fekadu acted the part of Emperor Menelik II. Anyone who saw and heard him sing or compose poetry was fascinated. The talent of this young man was exceptional. He was also well read in modern and ancient Ethiopian history. In his neighborhood, everyone thought that, one day, Fekadu Molla would become a great poet, playwright or actor.

After finishing fifth grade, Fekadu had planned to study mathematics at the Patriot School. But he got a job offer from the first public library and started working there instead. Everything was fine until, one day, the assistant minister of information fired him. Many speculate that it was after losing his employment that he became ill. However Fekadu himself thinks it was only depression. He claims he has doctors' letters to prove it.

Then, at other times, he thinks to himself, "That is how it happened. I was just starting to get better. My mother—God bless her—was taking me to the holy stream. I was getting better. But then I saw the dead bodies in the street. There were so many, I couldn't pass. Then I don't remember anything. My mother told me later that I was found lying there. Then they sent me to Emanuel Mental Hospital."

But he also says that the doctors, without proper evaluation, declared him crazy and unfit. Once he was branded crazy, no one took him seriously anymore. He knew he wasn't mentally ill, but who believed him.

◆-◆-◆

Whatever the reason, everyone just calls him "Fekadu Ebdu (Crazy)."

Fekadu spends every day near Saint George's Church in front of Menelik II Square. Often when passersby heard him sing, they stopped to listen. For the unemployed, this is a one-man show! Very recently Fekadu Molla had taken to singing a war song from the Battle of Adwa.

◆-◆-◆

Today, two girls come running by, laughing and calling, "Gashe Fekadu, Ebdu Fekadu." Fekadu Ebdu follows after them, running as they try to escape. These girls are terrified even seeing him from a distance. Though the boys claim not to be afraid, they also try to avoid him. If you look closely you can see the fear on their faces. Of course boys have to pretend to be brave.

Fekadu frightens all the children in the neighborhood. He gets angry because he doesn't like people to stare at him. Sometimes the children throw stones and hit him on his back and legs. When that happens, he is the one who runs. Any other person in his age group would be addressed with respect. Adults try to tell the children to stop. They say, "He doesn't harm anyone unless he is attacked." They say, "Who are your parents and how is it that they didn't teach you to respect your elders?"

Except for this unpleasantness from the children, Fekadu accepts his life. At least it gives him the freedom to express his feelings and to say anything he wants to, something that "normal" citizens can't do. And he wears anything he likes. When he wears shoes, his little toe can be seen through a hole with more holes on top. To him mixing the colors of his clothes or paying attention to little details like a normal person are too much of a bother. He wears green, yellow, red, black and white at the same time. These days, with things so bad, Fekadu has

Menelik's statue

taken to wearing green, yellow and red—colors of the Ethiopian flag. Some people wonder if he'll get in trouble with the authorities. But no one touches him. He has one bag. In it he carries everything he owns, along with needle and thread. He tears his clothes off of himself and then sits down and sews them back together.

So, he's crazy. Or is he? There are some who wonder if Fekadu Ebdu actually pretends to be crazy so that the officials will leave him alone to speak and act as he wants. But everyone can see that at times he himself doesn't even know what he is doing. Especially when he throws his clothes off and goes out naked, showing his private parts. Then they wonder, why don't they return him to Emanuel Mental Hospital?

Fekadu talks to the statue sometimes. Menelik stares back and looks as though he will gallop away any minute, jumping over the iron fence. "Look at him! I wish we could have a heart to heart talk and chat about everything that troubles me. Then I would not be like this ..."

Before finishing what he was saying, those two girls who always run by called to him. But this time, they called out "Gashe Fekadu."

He couldn't believe his ears. They called to him, treating him like an elder, addressing him with respect.

"Antu Gashe Fekadu!"

Even more respect! He turned around with a smile and the girls didn't run this time. "What did you say my daughter?"

Walking closer, Sergut said, "He doesn't look crazy at all. It looks as if he became a healthy normal person for a minute." Sergut is holding Bayuish on her arm in fear. It looks as if she is pinching her and biting her own lips. She didn't listen to Fekadu's question.

"What did you say?" He wanted to hear one more time that she addressed him with respect.

Sergut heard this time, but couldn't get out what she wanted, tripping over words and thoughts. If she repeated what she had said, she was afraid of making him upset and triggering his mental illness.

From a distance, some young men, Nesibu among them, saw the girls, but were not sure what was going on. They half expected crazy Fekadu to harm them. They came closer and, behind them, others straggled along.

Fekadu tried to encourage her. "God bless you, my daughter. And thank you. It has been quite a while since I have been addressed with respect like you have."

He continued, changing the subject. "When my father took me to—God save his soul—when he took me to attend Menelik School, every ethnic group was there. People were not divided like today. The son of rich and poor, Amhara, Gurage, Tigray, Wellega, Illubabor, Kotu and Guggi studied together. Sharing that experience itself was educational. It was not like today where they try to split everything into the lowest common denominator."

When Fekadu responded to something that no one had asked him, they all started laughing.

"Though Gashe Fekadu read what was not written, he articulates like a normal person. A crazy person is not crazy twenty-four hours. Rather there are times he is normal. He is holding a rounded plate that looks like a shield with a weaver's thread sticking out. He holds it like a patriot," Bayuish explains.

Nesibu disagrees. "What happened to you? Are you telling her to make him more crazy? If he throws the stick he is holding like a spear, he may hit her."

As they talked Fekadu walked carefully toward Sergut. They didn't move from where they were. When he moved toward them the rest of the young people moved closer to the girls. Looking down as he walked, Fekadu saw a chicken feather and put it in his hair.

Bayuish laughed heartily and said, "Now Gashe Fekadu is pretending to be a Red Indian from America."

"Questions and answers must be addressed turn by turn," Nesibu replied.

Fekadu asked, "Why did you jump in and interrupt me before I answered her? Didn't you hear me when I asked her what she said to me? Aren't you a student? You have an exercise book? Is your teacher also Signor Dimitri? Haven't they taught you the ABCs of communication—to listen to others while they are talking?"

While Sergut and Bayuish asked one question and received a thousand replies, they bowed their heads, but weren't frightened. Sergut thought to herself, "It is true that a crazy and independent-minded individual always speaks up." Of all the things he said, they remembered his few French words because that was a mark of being crazy. They thought anyone who was French educated was crazy, like Mr. Bezabeh and his younger brother Mr. Kifle.

Sergut stands, still grasping Bayuish's arm. She is wearing sandals, poking the ground with her big toe. She isn't following the conversation. By now, the young men, Nesibu and Seifu are listening to Fekadu with amusement. Sergut didn't know what to do. Instead of her, Bayuish became talkative. Sergut came in on the middle of a thought.

"Which eve? What celebration?"

"Perhaps Gashe Fekadu might have something on his mind. Otherwise he wouldn't have called it the eve of the celebration." said Seifu.

Sergut continued to listen to what Seifu was saying, forgetting Fekadu. "I guess no one thinks they are crazy. He seems to accept his illness ..."

Suddenly Fekadu shouted loudly, "Hey! Hey!," to get their attention as the crowd around began to grow. "You don't know about the great victory of the Battle of Adwa? Get thrown in a ditch!" Then, turning to the men on the edge of the crowd, "and you too get thrown in a ditch! Today men are no better than women. In fact, the women are better. I thought you knew about the Battle of Adwa, standing here in front of Menelik's statue. You should be pondering the sacrifices our people made. The celebration of the Battle of Adwa is for all people on earth. For Rastafarians, Africans, African Americans, Red Indians, Asians ... it is the celebration for all humanity. You understand it. I know."

The crowd was almost quiet.

He continued. "Is carrying your history book near Menelik's statue enough to commemorate the victory of our forefathers against the Italian invaders without thanking every one of us—Gondere, Agame, Shewe, Gojjame, Wollege, Gurage, Amhara? May everyone respect you because you are Ethiopian. Your civilized behavior, cooperating and living together in peace with each other, should merit something."

"Today on the eve of the celebration of the Battle of Adwa you should remember those who sacrificed for you. Just like those who become rich and poor, poor again and rich again, you should consider in your thoughts all those who sacrificed for you."

Sergut, Nesibu and Seifu didn't say what they were thinking, that they didn't want to listen to this talkative

Fekadu, that they had better things to do. Even when he was mixing all kinds of stories with each other, turning them upside down with endless metaphors, they politely listened. In fact, it looked like a meeting of the minds with all of these men and women and this man who was not crazy. So they didn't accuse him of wasting their time. There were others thinking that they wished to be crazy like Fekadu, to speak their minds.

He drifted off again into his own mind. Even though he met these youngsters wearing his green, yellow and red rags,

Emperor Menelik II
detail from a painting by the late G.F. Harris

Taitu 1890 A.D. Afework Tekle

pulling it off his head, using it to cover his face, he spoke his mind about the victory of the Battle of Adwa. He was also aware of the consequences of speaking up and was a little afraid. This man was not excluded from the beatings of soldiers because of his illness. Many like him lose their eyesight or become crippled after such beatings.

His thoughts got louder. "With my effort, Sergut and many young people may understand the victory of the Battle of Adwa. They look at me as if to say in one voice, 'I see!' Those traitors who specialize in snatching victory from the people don't understand the history of Ethiopia. Only because determined people fought constantly to preserve our independence, even those who hate us can enjoy the fruits of this victory. Although they are ready to sell the freedom and independence of their country to the highest bidder ..."

Seifu said, "He really gave us a piece of his mind, scolded us up to our necks. Can anyone say they believe that Gashe Fekadu is sick?"

Nesibu responded, "Perhaps it is better if you call him healthy crazy," pointing and showing Seifu. "Look at him! Look now," as crazy Fekadu snatched Sergut's books and threw them over the iron fence near the Menelik statue. Expecting a serious confrontation between Sergut and Fekadu, the rest of them rushed closer, afraid of the consequences.

Sergut said, "Oh! Gashe Fekadu, what did I do to you? How can I get back my books?" using the forms of respect.

He responded, "The reason I did that is that I want you to climb the iron fence, get down and jump in front of the statue to get a chance to greet kind, beloved (*emeye*) Menelik on the eve of the Battle of Adwa. Look at him standing alone. Don't you feel sorry for him, surrounded by an iron fence and locked in with an iron lock. It looks as if Menelik is the prisoner of the new government for this hundred-year celebration. He would gallop off and escape if they didn't lock the door, if they didn't take his shield and his spear. When this statue was first built, Menelik was on his horse carrying his shield and spear. During the Second World War when the Italians invaded Ethiopia and bombarded Addis Ababa, the statue was destroyed. After the fascists were expelled, Britain volunteered to repair the statue. They must have been farseeing when they decided to take his spear and shield to put in the London Museum. What is amazing to me is why the new government officials locked Menelik up. Why are they afraid of him? From whom are they trying to protect him? Whatever happened, the quarrel died down long ago."

Nesibu reminded him of the point. "But what did she do to you?"

"This is to remind you that I am mentally ill. Just now when I talk with you I don't want to confuse the public into thinking I am healthy. She has done nothing. Hey, but what is your name anyway?" Gashe Fekadu asked.

"Sergut, she is Sergut," said Bayuish with shyness or fear. "Sergute Saint George," using the affectionate form by adding an "e" to the end of her name. Bayuish, smiling at the same time at Gashe Fekadu, said, "You were named at the time and date of Saint George the patriot saint who marched with

Menelik at the Battle of Adwa. Even if no one saw him, many swear he was there."

"This book *Great Men* talks about Alexander the Great, Napoleon Bonaparte—but never talks about Menelik," said Nesibu. "It seems to me the man who shattered the conspiracy against African people, the man who started the beginning of the end of the colonial scheme by defeating the European colonial army at their own game should have been included in this book."

Fekadu replied, "Sergut, you're indeed unfortunate now that you have no book. So, jump down near the Menelik's statue with your beautiful smile and beautiful hair and open your eyes that look like bright stars."

"Just between you and me, you are not really crazy," answered Sergut, making it seem as though she spoke bitterly because he had thrown her book.

"But, really, how is she going to get her book? Who is going to get it for her?" said Bayuish with subdued anger.

The young men who heard her anger responded, in one voice, "It's easy!" And they continued, using poetry, saying

Crazy Fekadu, even if he falls
he won't get hurt, even if he fails,
it won't hurt him ...

They continued, joking and mocking the whole thing.

"While these young men are here, do you really think I was going to get it for you?" asked Fekadu.

"We can do it, we can do it," the young men boasted, swaggering around.

By now, the crowd was getting larger and larger. It looked as if a big show were going on in the square. Sergut and Bayuish pushed Nesibu forward. Nesibu started asking crazy Fekadu leading questions in response to which he started to rant and rave.

Sergut drew attention back to her books, pointing. She didn't want them forgotten.

Fekadu began directing, "You young men. Just like prisoners of war, raise your hands, turn your faces to Menelik's statue and grasp the fence with your hands. Then Sergut can put one of her legs on each of your shoulders—let her swing over. Then she can gather her books."

Emperor Menelik and His Army's Route from Addis Ababa to Adwa

የዓፄ ምኒልክና የሠራዊታቸው ጉዞ ወደ ሰሜን

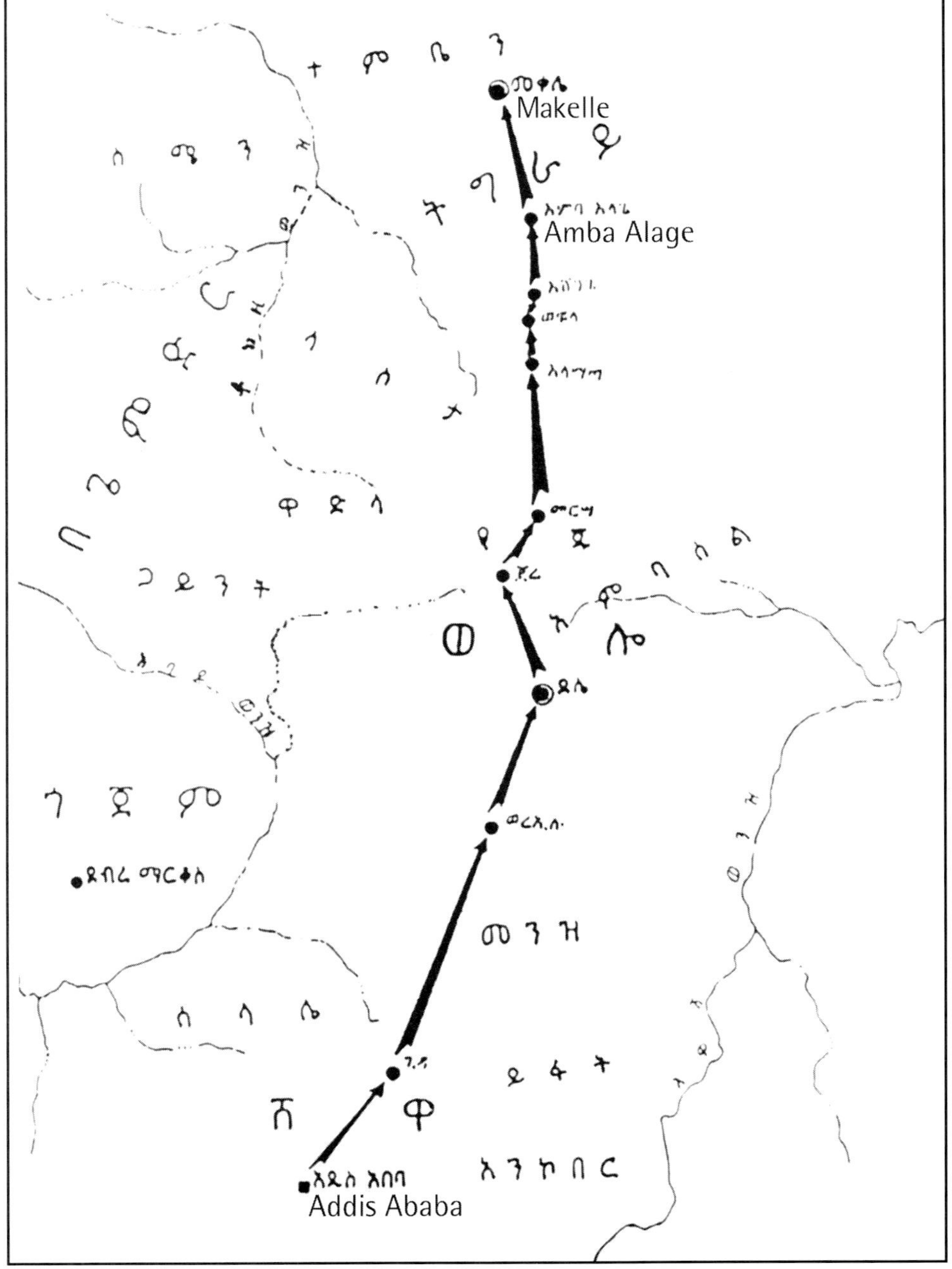

from *The Reign of Menelik II*, Gabre Selassie, pp.43-44

"She can also tell Menelik that she dropped in by accident so he doesn't suddenly jump from his horse. Even Mussolini's bomb didn't destroy him all together. What if he threw himself down and was damaged? Remember, this is your responsibility."

Sergut whispered to her friend, Bayuish, "I can't do it. My skirt will be torn. I never stepped on the shoulder of any man. So, so ... I trust these guys to get it for me." But she didn't have the courage to tell this to crazy Fekadu.

Because he was crazy he thought she didn't like his proposal. "Forget it Sergute Giorgis, because it is my responsibility. I, the crazy man, should jump this iron fence near this locked statue of Menelik that looks like a prison and get it for you. If I don't make it, don't worry. It is not my turn to march with Menelik, to smash the invaders for this hundred-year anniversary." As soon as he finished speaking he picked up his stick, holding it as though he were preparing to use a spear with his right arm and holding the old big dish like a shield with his left. The green, yellow and red rags on his head, he started to move forward when Seifu interrupted him: "No!, No!," stopping his plan.

"We will jump the fence, get her books and give them to her." But instead, they asked him to proceed with the story he started to tell about Adwa.

Soon even more people gathered. They all listened to Gashe Fekadu. Apparently, people began to take him seriously.

Staring at the crowd, holding and shaking his symbolic spear, eyes bugged out as though he were angry, he paused, took a big breath and began.

"This is what I learned from my father and this is what I inherited from him ..."

The number of people watching him continued to increase. As they moved closer, Fekadu got warmer and angrier, his mental temperature rising. He looked at the crowd and they seemed to get bigger and bigger in weight and size. His body started shaking. He was transforming before their eyes as though for a performance. He straightened his clothes. He smoothed and adjusted his head rag.

"... what he heard from his father and what I heard from my father and if all these government officials had heard it they wouldn't be harassing the poor, the cripples, the beggars."

Fasil Dawit 1995

families gathering wood at the edge of the camp

Before he finished what he was saying he sensed something from behind. Turning quickly to see if the security officers were finally trying to grab him, he saw, instead, Sergut and Nesibu.

Nesibu spoke. "When did colonialists civilize any country? Of all the things that surprise me is that those who make the most noise, claiming to be anti-colonialist and anti-imperialist, are competing to be first to embrace colonialism and imperialism. Most of the people who used to be progressive are now going backward. Would it not have been better to live in peace, with respect and equality with one's own people, instead of trying to divide us into the smallest unit?"

When Nesibu said this, Fekadu—not to be forgotten and to remind them of his existence—continued with his chorus of "... my father told me. Let me tell you what my father told me. My father was very young even for the Battle of Maichew, needless to say for the Battle of Adwa. He was born perhaps thirty-five years after the Battle of Adwa. He went to Maichew following his father. My grandfather was a soldier of the heroic leader Dejazmatch Basha Aboye who was killed in that battle. My grandfather recounted what he saw, not what he heard from *his* father."

"I just remembered the reason why these soldiers don't like the gathering of the poor to celebrate the hundredth anniversary of the Battle of Adwa. They don't want to see the poor with ragged clothes, some of them blind, some of them crippled, the rest of them poor like me."

"At that time when Menelik was going to meet the challenge of the Italians, every one of the poor beggars followed him. After the victory, even in Harrar, the people made memorials to him, like the hospital the Russians donated. Not respecting human beings—hating them—especially those who are blind, insulting them, even the village dog barks at a person like me. He wanted to destroy all kinds of government. That is why I wish Menelik's soul to be blessed in heaven."

"'Great Men.' I should have told that Gashe Paulos who wrote it in his book. Which Paulos? The son of Nogno! Nogno!? Yes, he might do that. When my supervisor fired me from my job, Gashe Paulos tried to support me."

from *The Graphic*, April 11, 1896 New York, New York

the Italian defeat at Adwa: the camp of the Abyssinians as seen from the Zalla Hill

"The memory of the people of Ethiopia should not be for sale," said Seifu, interrupting.

Sergut wanted to hear more. "Yes, I remember that book. It talked about the Battle of Adwa, the leader of the Italian army, General Baratieri, returned to his country. In a note written, according to an Italian journalist, men, women children, old people, cripples and beggars attacked them in hand to hand combat—according to General Baratieri's documentation. "

"He didn't mention my grandfather," said crazy Fekadu. "They never met, because my grandfather died when I was young. Paulos earned his living as a paperboy, selling newspapers. In fact, when I think of it, he was also selling a notebook to help you learn the Ethiopic alphabet and a prayer book published by Tesfa Gebre Selassie, the first Ethiopian publisher."

A bearded man joined in. "Oh! Menelik, celebrating his coronation in Entoto Mariam Church and on the second day celebrating Empress Taitu's coronation, marched to Adwa. He was assured the victory was his."

Fekadu interrupted. "Oh, no! That won't do. After Menelik and Taitu celebrated their coronation, they prayed and started their long journey to Tigray. The thing I vividly remember even now is that Menelik's army started the expedition after they completed prayers at Entoto Mariam Church. That journey—from Addis Ababa to Adwa, 1,060 kilometers—was spectacular by itself. Young and old, men and women, crippled and healthy, Christian and Moslem, every nationality behind the leader of their region went marching to the front. The chattering of the soldiers echoed from one end to the other. What I didn't forget is all those people including donkeys, mules and horses traveling with them. When the way was narrow, those in front cut trees in the thick jungle, removed obstacles and opened a path for the expedition. It looked as if everyone left their village to move to another place."

"The suffering along the way was terrible. My grandfather's face would suddenly change when he remembered how people died even before they had a chance to fight the enemy. My grandfather's memory of the musicians who accompanied them was vivid. He would sing me their war song. " And

Fekadu started to ramble through the song and other snatches of poetry.

One person touched by Fekadu's speech and poetry asked, "But are you really crazy or not?" He looked embarrassed, realizing what had slipped from his mouth. The crowd, ignoring him, urged Fekadu to go on.

"My grandfather used to say to me, 'You can't imagine how we served the wishes of Menelik in this battle. We followed, even without ammunition to fight the enemy. Everyone was determined to kill at least one Italian invader, even if they were going to die in the service of their emperor.' As everyone knows, Menelik was the emperor who never forgot to reward his followers. Menelik gave land to my grandfather—right on the plot where the present water resource authority resides."

The Grazmatch from Makelle broke in, introduced himself and said he had been a food supply officer during the second Italian invasion at the Battle of Maichew. He pointed out that his title was given him by His Imperial Majesty Haile Selassie.

He took up the story. "During the battle of Amba Alage the defeated Italian soldiers escaped and traveled on foot for six days to join the Italian army at the fortress at Makelle. Earlier the Italian military command had attacked the Abyssinians, expecting them to run, but instead faced hand-to-hand combat. Some of them were hurt badly. But the Italians wanted to get revenge for their disgraceful defeat at the Battle of Amba Alage. So they gathered their forces at the fortress of Makelle to try one more time. But Like Mequas Abate, Ras Makonnen and Ras Alula attacked the Italians at their Makelle fortress. After their defeat at Makelle, the Italian army fled and started to build a fortress at Adwa." Grazmatch explained that he had to jump in—just to make the story unfold in an orderly fashion.

Another older person told how the Italians built their fortress. Gashe Setegn started to tell the story he had heard from the older folks. This man did not need to explain where he came from. The way he spoke clearly indicated his origin. He could not see any difference between being an Ethiopian and an Amhara. He said, "I hope everyone here respects my brother from Makelle who just spoke. It looks as if God saved Fekadu. He is okay. Everyone here is blessed by almighty God." He was a little afraid the crowd would leave, bored by similar speeches.

However, turn by turn, one by one, many spoke and transmitted what they heard from their grandfathers. It looked as if people were enjoying the celebration of the hundredth year anniversary of the Battle of Adwa already.

Though they were often distracted, Sergut, Bayuish and Nesibu paused to listen to the speeches. Even some of the soldiers near the square had come to listen to them.

"The Italians made the fortress of Adwa much stronger than the fortress at Makelle. Even the birds could not be seen, much less armed soldiers. The design was also very different and modern. The fortress was three meters deep like Makelle; this one was four meters deep and built with hard stones. The fortress was also forty meters across and on top, thorny wires and broken bottles were cemented to cut the hands and legs of any intruder. The Italians' shrewd tactics didn't stop there. Since the Italians knew that the soldiers of Atse Menelik didn't wear shoes, all the roads were covered with sharp bits of wood, thorns and sharp wire rolled into a booby trap. Because the Italians knew the soldiers would use their swords to cut the rolled wire, when they did, the sharp wood would be released to stab them. The Italians' trick was to kill as many Abyssinians as they could before they even arrived near the fortress."

Fekadu jumped up and down, interrupting. "Menelik was no fool. Since he knew some of these tricks from Amba Alage and Makelle, he prepared a different strategy. Of course, the Italians were sure of their superiority over the Ethiopians. They were conceited and it never occurred to them that their enemy could change fighting methods. This time Menelik gave the order not to attack but to wait for further instructions. This was what I was told by my father, from his father."

"Everyone must agree that Gashe Fekadu is not crazy after all. If he is crazy everyone of us are crazy, too. Let anyone raise his or her hand who thinks he's crazy?" said Sergut. "Let the doctor who examined him bring proper evidence and then we will not accept his conclusion."

Even before Gashe Fekadu could finish telling the story, a bearded university student said "My sister is right."

This discussion spread through the crowd, which soon became restless, ready to disperse—when Fekadu spoke loudly over them, continuing his lesson. "When Menelik arrived at Adwa, he put his command in the middle of five hills. However,

Abyssinian soldiers

the Italians were looking through their telescope. Does anyone here know what General Baratieri said?" he asked.

Sergut quoted the general, reciting: "It looks like these Africans are planning to exterminate all Europeans."

People applauded Sergut with admiration for knowing this fact. Then Gashe Fekadu began rambling on about Sergut Saint George and why she was here on this day, confusing one issue with the other. Sergut, not knowing how to handle him, turned back to her conversation with Bayuish.

"The voluntary forces of Atse Menelik were lively in the costumes of many different regions. Some wore brightly colored overcoats. Others wore lion skins, holding in their hands shields and spears. To motivate these fighters, musicians were present on the battlefield. The priests were there, too. In the early morning, just when the sun was coming out, the Italian commanders looked out from their fortress. General Albertone later told how terrified the Italian army was at the sight of Menelik's army.

"Of all things, my grandfather was called to see Menelik himself. A few days before the beginning of the war we were ordered to cut big trees to make a fortress. My father was also called to see Menelik like my grandfather. The day was the ninteenth, Saint Gabriel's Day, in Makelle Enda Yesus Church—burned by the Italians."

One old man interrupted. "When your father was received by Menelik, he was young. You didn't tell us who else he saw there. Didn't you find *my* grandfather?"

"I think you are making fun of me. At that time, none of us knew each other," said Fekadu.

"What did Menelik say to the older people and children?" the man put in.

"Maybe it is better if you speak. Tell us. Unless I tell you the story by acting just like the actors at Hager Fiker Theater, I may not be able to tell my story. Is there anybody who opposes that? I want to wear my clothes exactly like Menelik and act like him." Fekadu then put his hand in his bag and took out a folder. He also pulled out a balloon and blew it up.

Seifu noticed what Fekadu was doing. "Look at Gashe Fekadu. He has put something on his face, put a ring on his finger and an earring on his right ear."

Most of the audience struggled to keep themselves from laughing as Fekadu Molla unbuttoned the folder held together by a thread and tied white fabric around his head. They burst out when he began trying to imitate the dignified walk of Emperor Menelik. Even the armed soldier started laughing when he saw crazy Fekadu pretending to imitate Menelik giving a speech.

"The Italians who disrespect the black people and who believe that *habesha* are not equal to Europeans came to conquer us. They want us to become their servants and take our lands. But they were not successful until now. This conceited effort and empty pride must be punished on the battlefield. Our courage and dedication to our freedom and independence are considered empty valor without substance to them. Though we have defeated them many times, they never learn that our army is dedicated to driving them out of our country. Now, in Adwa, they are waiting for us to storm the fortress and attack them. This I received from my intelligence officer. But I am not going to do that. God is my witness. I will not allow my soldiers to become a target for their cannons. I have different methods. I know the Italians also have spies. Because many people died during our efforts at Amba Alage and Makelle, as a result, our strategy now is new and different.

"Fighting all of us is unacceptable. No one should betray the whole nation because we quarrel among ourselves. When I was in Mersa, Dejazmatch Guangul Zegeye sent me a message asking forgiveness for his earlier mistakes. Without recounting all the crimes he committed, I forgave him and he has kept his land and his title. Because I gave my word in front of God and to all of you, he is now my loyal soldier.

"I don't know anyone who prefers to fight for the enemy against our country. Some patriotic Ethiopians, whom the Italians hired to spy, have already informed me as to their military plan. Though these patriots prefer to fight on our side, I told them to go back and inform me of the Italians' activities. It took me quite a long time to persuade them that they are more valuable to us there. Knowing the Italian command's strategy and tactics has helped us change ours. They are waiting in their fortress for us to come running to storm them. They have only to stick their heads up from their trenches and shoot their cannons and guns where they are

view from the north of the fortified Italian camp at Adwa, captured by the Abyssinians

from *The Graphic*, April 11, 1896 New York, New York

protected. When we have attacked them in the open they run away.

"So I decided on a campaign of misinformation—that most of our soldiers are hungry, tired and ready to retreat. Especially because of diseases, they are unable to fight. The Italians believed a story of mutiny among my soldiers. I know it is not right to fabricate such lies in front of my God and all of my people. But since they came to invade our country, I hope the almighty God will forgive me—because it is my duty and responsibility to drive the enemy from my land. The Italians never thought we had brains like them to plan strategy and tactics. They never imagined that we could make spies of chosen informers work for us. I don't like this spying business. I know the almighty God will forgive my sin of spying on other human beings. But the plan of the Italian command is to invade our country, take our land and change our religion by force.

"I have prayed for peace and cooperation with the Italians, but no amount of kindness will make them stop their aggression. So we have to stop them in the only language they understand—force. Even though most of my Hamasien children who are members of the Italian army want to fight side by side with us, I told them to help us by staying with the Italian army and informing us of their intentions and troop movements.

"Because Mohammed Abdulrahiem was suspected of being sympathetic to Ethiopia, he was removed as governor of the district. The Italians replaced him with his brother who was known to them because he brought them vegetables and meat. God is my witness—I did not ask him to do anything. However, he gave us details of Italian troops leaving the port of Massawa. He followed them and found reliable messengers to go to Ras Alula and also be spies.

"My wish is that the Italians would come out of their fortress at Adwa. I don't want my soldiers to be slaughtered by Italian cannon. So I will lure the Italians out so my soldiers can attack them from three different directions. Knowing when they are coming out is very important.

"Now, you children, mothers, young and old and especially beggars, go near the Italian fortress and beg for food and drink. Tell them that Menelik's soldiers are deserting and going

Emperor Menelik II wearing traditional head covering

back south, that most of them are sick, that many have died of malaria and other diseases. Tell them the soldiers are leaving for Shoa. I will assign someone to help you coordinate your assignment."

Gashe Fekadu was abruptly interrupted by the gentleman from Makelle and, following him, a gentleman from Menze who both agreed with crazy Fekadu. Everything they had heard—"not even leaving one thing out"—from their own grandfathers was the same. The Battle of Adwa was decided not only because of the valor of the Ethiopian soldiers but also because of the wise leadership of Menelik and all his generals. The Italian military command was consistently given false information about strategy, tactics and the morale of Menelik's soldiers. The spying involved many people, especially the military. These three respectable older citizens spoke and exchanged their opinions, imparting much new knowledge to the crowd. Then they all started singing a war song from even before the Battle of Adwa. They finished to thunderous applause and whistles.

A passing priest, wearing his white turban and black clothes, stopped, holding a cross wrapped in yellow cloth. He raised the cross to the people saying, "That is right! That is right! Don't you remember how the women would compose such poetry?" Saying this he went to where Gashe Fekadu was standing and planted his feet. Then, wriggling under his clothes, he put his hand in and took out a book.

"*Besmeab wold we menfus kidus ahadu,*" he blessed the gathering crowd. "Yes, it is written here. We love the truth of a book in our hand. It is not enough to say that Menelik won the battle because of his spies. Even though many of us are not educated in a classic modern educational system, those who fought themselves have written and preserved it. It is true that no one had used disinformation-misinformation tactics before. But Menelik was a very wise leader."

"He respected all his advisors and listened to them attentively, addressing each regional leader with the words of respect—sir, *getoch*—used equal to equal. Like this he discussed everything with Ras Alula, Ras Mangesha, Ras Wole, Ras Abate—for this was the war that decided whether Ethiopia would remain an independent nation or become a colony of a European country. This was also considered a defeat for the British, the French, the Germans and the European colonialists who participated in the Berlin Conference.

Empress Taitu with Ethiopian braids (sheruba)

"The commander of the Italian army, General Baratieri, in the evening of Yekatit 21 (Ethiopian calendar), ordered his soldiers to attack. However, because of the rain they could not move out until the next day. General Dabormida occupied one mountain. General Arimondi was on one side and Albertone on the other.

"As soon as they heard the Italian army moving, Ras Makonnen led his Harrar troops and marched to fight the enemy. Ras Mikael leading the Wello troops seized that mountain. King Tekle Haimanot with his Gojjam troops moved fast and reached near to the Italian fortress. Ras Mangesha Yohannes with his Tigray troops blocked the path of General Albertone's troops. General Albertone had planned to capture Abba Garima in Adwa but couldn't catch him. Menelik and Taitu, leading their troops, along with Dejazmatch Balcha and his Gurage troops made for the other flank, fast, securing a stretch of thirteen kilometers. The Oromo horsemen, covering the thirteen kilometers and circling a stream, deprived the Italian armies of water.

"Through all the melée, musicians sang motivational songs: *ere gifu buzza ... ere gifu buzza* (the crime is too much ... the crime is too much). And the clergy prayed loudly, begging their mighty God to give Menelik's army the strength and power to defeat the invading Italian army.

"In the middle of the night Ras Mangesha Yohannes's troops attacked General Albertone's troops at Enda Kidane Meheret. They fought the whole night. At 7:00 in the morning General Dabormida's troops started to move to assist General Albertone's. However, the road was blocked by the Ethiopian troops. General Dabormida changed his route, but the mountains were in between. Many of his soldiers died fighting.

"By that time, General Baratieri, leading his troops on horseback, arrived near Dabormida and saw many wounded Italians retreating from Enda Kidane Mariam. Now, Baratieri trembled with fear. He finally knew the power of Menelik.

"If this had only been written by Ethiopians, people could say the author was partial to his people. However, Baratieri and Albertone returned to Italy after being released by Menelik and wrote extensive accounts of their humiliation. What is amazing is that when Baratieri gave orders for his officers to fire their guns and cannon, Menelik's soldiers ran straight ahead with their swords raised to kill their enemies hand to hand. It took only a few hours for the heroic Ethiopian combatants to silence the cannons. After that, the many dead bodies of Italians became dinner for the vultures.

"There were many prisoners, but Menelik ordered that they not be chained. Generals Arimondi, Dabormida and Gallioni died in battle. On the Ethiopian side, two outstanding heroes of Adwa—Dejazmatch Basha Aboye and Fitawrari Gebiehu—died as well. All this is also written by the Italians. General Baratieri, the Italian commander and his second in command, Albertone, were taken prisoner.

"Though the victory belonged to Menelik, this wise leader knew that the battle was won with the help of many gallant fighters—including the wise leadership of the regional leaders and the will of God.

"He was gracious and generous in pardoning his enemies. He said, 'they are human beings like us and shouldn't be punished severely just because they are our enemies. Just as my sons and daughters are buried in a religious ceremony with the blessing of Abune Matewos, the personal belongings of our enemy dead must be gathered and sent to Rome for their families'. The burial of high-ranking Italian officers was performed in the presence of His Imperial Majesty Emperor Menelik II of Ethiopia and other dignitaries. Let Europe and the world see the kindness of His Majesty—that even the enemies who came to invade his country are treated equally on their deathbeds.

"Menelik then ordered the Secretary of Pen to write a letter to the Italian government and the families of the prisoners and the dead saying that he had never wanted to go to war with the Italian government. As all his letters and pleading had fallen on deaf ears, he had had no choice but to defend his country from the aggressor. He dictated, 'Until the last hour, I assigned my brother Prince Makonnen to do everything in his power to negotiate a peaceful settlement of our quarrel. However, the Italians believed that might was right and invaded our country. God the Almighty and the Powerful saw the wicked intentions of the Italian government and blessed our troops so that we became victorious. Still we are very sorry for all the dead and wounded. Such a catastrophe could have been avoided had the Italian government listened to our pleas for peace.'"

Finally the priest ended, completely out of breath. He looked as if he had been preaching the gospel. His eyes brimmed with tears and the crowd was filled with emotion. He whispered, after a long pause, "... This book in my hand was written by Afework Gebre Yesus Zebhere Zege when he was a student in Italy during the Battle of Adwa. This book is also a detailed book about the Battle of Adwa." Opening the book as though he were opening his bible, he continued, "The victory of Adwa was secured through the sacrifices of all nationalities and ethnic groups of Ethiopia." Quoting Afework, he intoned "The Shoan horse riders, the infantry of Gojjam, the Amhara tacticians and the skinny Tigreans, the speedy Begemdir who is faster than a tiger ... ." he went on, ending in a sigh.

Finally, he regained his breath, though only a murmur had gone through the crowd. "It seems that with seemingly good intentions, powerful people try to create conflict among us. The ancestors of the present-day Ethiopians who fought and won this battle come from every corner. So shouldn't we learn something from this? Let us respect each other and listen to each other. Our ancestors were wise and patient, not letting differences of ethnicity, region, nationality, wealth or education keep them from building something fine."

Fekadu finally spoke up with a few words to tease the priest. "Father, you should advise the people to minimize their praying, worshipping and leaving everything to God. As a peasant saying goes, 'If a donkey says God will protect me and goes into the forest in the middle of the night, he will send her a hungry hyena.' As everyone can see, leaving everything to Him may make us end up like this donkey. Unless our people realize that they will get nothing except by identifying their goals and working to reach them, then we have learned nothing at all today. Do you remember the ancient Ethiopian priest who once said God helps only those who help themselves?"

After he said this, he turned his face to Nesibu, Sergut, Seifu and Bayuish. It looks as if he is trying to take something important out of his bag. Yes, he is pulling out an old notebook. In this notebook he had composed some poetry for the one-hundred-year anniversary of the victory at the Battle of Adwa. Fekadu Molla, almost in a trance, recited his poetry like the actor he may have once aspired to be.

After finishing, eyes wet with emotion, silence reigned among the audience. As he stood still there, Sergut and Nesibu said "Long live the victory of the Battle of Adwa!" Following them, the assembled chanted three times, "Long live the victory of the Battle of Adwa! Long live the victory of the Battle of Adwa! Long live the victory of the Battle of Adwa!"

After the crowd melted away, Fekadu, Sergut, Nesibu, Bayuish and Seifu stood silently, standing close by the statue of Menelik.

translated by Fassil Yirgu
adapted by Pamela S. Brown

Selected Readings

for How Africa Defeated Europe

Ayele Bekerie

Asante, S.K.B. 1977. *Pan-African Protest: West Africa and the Italo-Ethiopian Crisis, 1934–1941*. London: Longman Group Ltd.

Azikiwe, Nnamadi. 1968. *Renascent Africa*. London: Frank Cars and Co.

Campbell, Horace. 1987. *Rasta and Resistance from Marcus Garvey to Walter Rodney*. Trenton: Red Sea Press.

Clarke, John Henrik, ed. 1971. *Harlem U.S.A.* Berlin: Seven Sea Publishers.

Del Boca, Angelo. 1969. *The Ethiopian War 1935–1941*. Chicago: University of Chicago Press.

DuBois, WEB. 1935. "Inter-Racial Implications of the Ethiopian Crisis: A Negro View," *Foreign Affairs*, vol. 14, no. 1 (October 1935): 82–92.

Essien-Udom, E.U. 1969. *Black Nationalism: A Search for an Identity in America*. New York: Dell Publishing Co.

Foner, Phillip S., ed. 1978. *Paul Robeson Speaks: Writings, Speeches, Interviews 1918–1974*. New York: Bunner and Mazel.

Garvey, Amy J., ed. 1969. *Philosophy and Opinions of Marcus Garvey*. New York: Atheneum.

Geiss, Immanuel. 1974. *The Pan-African Movement*. London: Methuen and Co. Ltd.

Hansberry, Leo William. 1981. *Pillars in Ethiopian History: African History Notebook*. Volume 1. Edited by Joseph Harris. Washington, DC.: Howard University Press.

Harris, Joseph E. 1994. *African American Reactions to War in Ethiopia, 1936–1941*. Baton Rouge, La.: Louisiana State University Press.

Houston, Drusilla Dunjee. 1985. *Wonderful Ethiopians of the Ancient Cushite Empire*. Baltimore: Black Classic Press.

Huggins, Willis N., and John G. Jackson. 1973. *An Introduction to African Civilizations with Main Currents in Ethiopian History*. New York: Negro University Press.

Jacobs, Virginia Lee. 1985. *Roots of Rastafari*. San Diego: Slawson Communications.

Magubane, Bernard M. 1987. *The Ties That Bind: African-American Consciousness of Africa*. Trenton: Africa World Press.

Marcus, Harold. 1994. *The Life and Times of Menelik II: Ethiopia 1844–1913*. Trenton: Red Sea Press.

Markakis, John. 1974. *Ethiopia: Anatomy of a Traditional Polity*. Oxford: Clarendon Press.

Mazrui, Ali A., and Michael Tidy. 1986. *Nationalism and New States in Africa: From About 1935 to the Present*. London: Heinemann.

Mekuria, Tekle Tsadik. 1893 (Amharic). *Atse Menelikena Yethiopia Andenat*. Addis Ababa: Kuraz Publishers.

Nkrumah, Kwame. 1970. *Africa Must Unite*. New York: International Publishers.

Pakenham, Thomas. 1991. *The Scramble for Africa 1876–1912*. New York: Random House.

Prouty, Chris. 1986. *Empress Taytu and Menelik II Ethiopia 1883–1910*. Trenton: Red Sea Press.

Rodney, Walter 1981. *How Europe Underdeveloped Africa*. Washington, DC.: Howard University Press.

Rogers, J.A. 1982. *The Real Facts About Ethiopia*. Baltimore: Black Classic Press.

Sbacchi, Alberto. 1985. *Ethiopia Under Mussolini: Fascism and the Colonial Experience*. London: Zed Books Ltd.

Scott, William R. 1993. *The Sons of Sheba's Race: African-Americans and the Italo-Ethiopian War, 1935-1941*. Bloomington: Indiana University Press.
Tamrat, Tadesse. 1972. *Church and State in Ethiopia 1270–1527*. Oxford: Clarendon Press.
Tibebu, Teshale. 1995. *The Making of Modern Ethiopia 1896–1974*. Trenton: Red Sea Press.
Trimingham, J.S. 1952. *Islam in Ethiopia*. London: Oxford University Press.
Yenesaw, Asras. 1951 (in Amharic). *Tebe Aksum Menu Ante?* Addis Ababa: Commerce Printing Press.
Zewde, Bahru. 1991. *A History of Modern Ethiopia 1855–1974*. Addis Ababa: Addis Ababa University Press.

References

for Adwa and Menelik

Teshale Tibebu

1. Count Gleichen, *With the Mission to Menelik, 1897.* London: Edward Arnold, 1898, 152.

2. Dorothy Hammond and Alta Jablow, *The Africa That Never Was*, Prospect Heights, Ill.: Waveland Press, 1992, 97.

3. Herbert Vivian, *Abyssinia Through the LionLand to the Court of the Lion of Judah*, New York: Negro Universities Press, 1969, 248.

4. Emperor Tewodros cited in Pankhurst, "Ethiopia and Somalia," in Ajayi ed., *UNESCO General History of Africa*, vol. 6, 397.

5. Tewodros II's letter to Kaiser Wilhelm 1, cited in Zewde Gebre Selassie, *Yohannes IV: A Political Biography*, 1975, 248.

About the Contributors

Ayele Bekerie teaches African Studies and is a visiting professor at Cornell University in Ithaca, New York. He is the author of published articles and presents numerous papers at African and African-American academic conferences.

Fasil Dawit is an artist living in Washington DC. A former head of the Graphic Arts Division of the Ethiopian Television Center in Addis Ababa, his works are on permanent display at the Ethiopian Postal Museum. He created original paintings for a 1970s documentary about Adwa and has shown at galleries in Ethiopia and the US.

Tsegaye Gabre-Medhin is Ethiopia's Poet Laureate and resides in Addis Ababa, Ethiopia. He has produced many plays and is well known as a playwright and social commentator as well as a poet. He travels internationally to conferences and presentations.

Donald N. Levine is the Peter B. Ritzma Professor at the University of Chicago and a distinguished sociologist whose specialty is Ethiopia. He is best known for his books about Ethiopia, *Wax and Gold* and *Greater Ethiopia*.

Richard K.P. Pankhurst is Ethiopia's foremost historian, the former head of the Ethiopian Institute in Addis Ababa and resides in Ethiopia. He is best known for his book *Economic History of Ethiopia* and has written numerous other works on literature, the arts, social movements and so on.

Amare Tegbaru is a historical novelist and lives in Stockholm, Sweden. Author of the two-volume historical novel about Ethiopia from 1935 to 1974, *Yandit Medir Lijotch*, he has written numerous articles and poetry in his native language, Amharic.

Afework Tekle, Ethiopia's Master Artist, lives in Addis Ababa. A prolific painter for almost 40 years, he is known internationally for his stained glass windows at African Hall, headquarters in Addis Ababa of the Organization of African Unity. He exhibits his work in Africa, Europe and the United States.

Teshale Tibebu teaches African History at Temple University in Philadelphia. He has written numerous papers and articles for academic journals and for presentation at conferences and is well known among African scholars. His book, *The Making of Modern Ethiopia 1896–1974*, was published in 1995.

Fikre Tollosa is a poet, playwright and teaches at Columbia Pacifica University in San Rafael, California and is on the editorial board of the Ethiopian business magazine *Bir.* Known for his plays and poetry in Ethopia and the US, he has performed in Russia, Germany and other European countries.